500 Things Every Technology Professional Needs to Know

500 Things Every Technology Professional Needs to Know

Published by TechRepublic
ISBN 1-933711-21-3
Printed August 2006

Disclaimer

The information contained herein has been obtained from sources believed to be reliable. CNET Networks, Inc. disclaims all warranties as to the accuracy, completeness, or adequacy of such information. CNET Networks, Inc. shall have no liability for errors, omissions, or inadequacies in the information contained herein or for the interpretations thereof. The reader assumes sole responsibility for the selection of these materials to achieve its intended results. The opinions expressed herein are subject to change without notice.

TechRepublic
1630 Lyndon Farm Court
Louisville, KY 40223
Tel.: 1.800.217.4339
Online Customer Support:
http://techrepublic.custhelp.com/

August 2006
B102

Credits

Director, Business Technologies
Carmen Barrett

Senior Editor
John Sheesley

Operations Manager
Marilyn Bryan

Graphic Artist
Kimberly Wright

Copy Editor
Julie Tonini

Promotions Manager
Megan Hancock

Customer Support Manager
Elisa Suiter

Customer Care Specialist
DeeDee Quinones

Foreword

There is so much to know when you're an IT professional that it's almost impossible to know everything there is about the field. You may not even know what you don't know you should know. That's where *500 Things Every Technology Professional Needs to Know* comes in.

Broken down into easy-to-understand lists, this book distills some of the most important things you need to know when you're an IT professional. 500 Things builds on TechRepublic's well-known 10 Things series. It covers such areas as:

- Windows XP
- Applications
- Windows Server 2003
- Linux
- Hardware
- Web Development

Quick hitting. Easy to understand. Looking through this book, you'll amaze yourself about what you already know about being an IT professional, how much you've forgotten in your day-to-day routine, and how much you have yet to learn.

500 Things Every Technology Professional Needs to Know

Windows XP

Applications

Windows Server 2003

Linux

Hardware

Web Development

Windows XP

10 things you should do to improve every new Windows PC

By Mark W. Kaelin

Getting a new PC, whether it is at work or at home, is one of those "makes you smile" moments. Just like the "6 Million Dollar Man" we all want better, stronger, and faster. However, every new PC that crosses your path is in need of a few tweaks. This article lists 10 enhancements you should make to every new PC, no matter whether it is a workstation or the family media computer. These tweaks will bring out the best in your new PC and give you a solid foundation for future applications and operating system updates.

1. Prepare it for the Internet.

The first step should always be to implement the necessary security measures required for connecting it to the Internet. For office workstations and PCs installed by network administrators, much of this preliminary work will have already been done, but for home PCs these steps are essential. Connecting a new PC to the Internet before taking the proper security steps will be construed by the nefarious citizens of the Internet as an invitation to infect your PC with a virus, worm, or Trojan horse. The scariest part of that scenario: the infection is likely to take place within 12 minutes of connecting to the Internet.

2. Turn on ClearType and adjust Desktop settings.

One of the first things I do when I sit down at a new Windows PC for the first time is activate the ClearType effect located on the Display Properties control panel. To get to the right control, open the Control Panel and then open the Display Properties control panel. From there, navigate to the Appearance tab and click the Effects button.

Click the second check box for smoothing font edges and choose the ClearType option. Click OK a few times and you should see the fonts displayed much more crisply on the screen. For tired eyes, like mine, this can literally save you a few headaches, especially if you have to stare at a monitor screen all day. Once you install the Microsoft PowerToys (see #9) you can adjust the ClearType settings to achieve a more personalized display.

This is also where you would adjust the size of the Windows icons, choose whether to allow the screen contents to show while dragging, specify themes, and designate font style and size. Those are all personal choices and will vary, but for those of us who look at the screen all day, these setting must be adjusted.

One important thing I do is change the background color for text areas in Windows. The default is white, but that is often too bright for me. I change it to off white to reduce the intensity and the eye strain it causes. It is a small change, but I think it makes a big difference.

3. Configure file system.

Sometimes large software companies like Microsoft take on a motherly role by configuring their software to protect us from ourselves. This is the case with the default manner in which the file system is displayed in Windows Explorer—system files are hidden, file extensions are hidden, and big icons are displayed instead of a detailed list. Some of these settings may be a matter of personal preference, but if you are going to truly know your PC and the Windows OS up and down, front to back, you will need to see all the information about a file displayed in every listing you see.

To set up the file display to your liking, open Windows Explorer and navigate to Tools | Folder Options on the menu and then to the View tab. Next, you want to look down the list of checkboxes and radio buttons to find the one that says Show Hidden Files And Folders. I also recommend you click the checkboxes next to:

- Display The Contents Of The System Folders
- Display The Full Path In The Address Bar

You should also uncheck the boxes next to:

- Hide Extensions For Know File Types
- Hide Protected Operating System Files

Revealing the protected OS system files can be dangerous if you are one who likes to delete files and ask questions later, but as long as you are careful, I think the benefits outweigh the risks.

Once you get the folder view the way you want it, you should click the Apply To All Folders button to make the view common to all folders.

4. Set screen resolution and Hz and DPI.

Once again, this suggestion may stem from my aging eyes, but the general concept is sound for all new PCs. Go to the Control Panel and open the Display Properties. While you may want to change the Appearance or activate a Screen Saver, my concern is with the Settings tab. The resolution determined by the install process (includes any OS) may not be the best resolution for your hardware or for your eyes.

For LCD monitors, the resolution settings should match the native resolution of the monitor itself. The native resolution is easy to determine: it is the maximum resolution the LCD monitor can actually display.

For CRT monitors, the resolution settings should be set to values that are most comfortable to your eyes. For monitor sizes of 17 inches or more that would most likely mean settings of at least 1024 X 768. However, the actual settings available are determined by your hardware, which includes not only the monitor but also the video card.

Perhaps even more important than the resolution are the settings for Dots Per Inch (DPI) and the Screen Refresh Rate. These controls are under the Advanced button of the Display Properties. The DPI, found under the General tab, determines how large the display fonts will be on a Windows PC. The default is 96 DPI, but at resolutions above 1024 X 768, I prefer a DPI of 120.

The Screen Refresh control is found under the Monitor tab. Your monitor will determine what settings are available here, but for CRTs I prefer a relatively high refresh rate of 85 Hz. Although you may not notice it, the monitor screen is constantly flickering. This flicker can give you a headache and make your eyes hurt if it is too slow, especially with CRTs. LCDs are a little different. They are usually limited to 60 Hz, but because they use a different technology, the strain to the eyes is much less pronounced.

5. Activate Windows.

At some point during the setup process you will likely be asked to activate Windows. (In Linux you would similarly be asked to register your particular distribution.) This is a good time to get that out of the way. Taking this step assures your operating system is legitimate and opens up a new set of support features, including community forums and FAQs.

6. Copy over browser shortcuts.

For many of us, our list of favorite Web sites is a reflection of our lives. It is more than a mere list of places on the Word Wide Web; it is our connection to a dynamic virtual world. Furthermore, once a link is placed into your browser, you don't really have to worry about remembering what can often be a cryptic URL. However, because you don't have to remember, you may actually forget what it is. This is why porting over your browser favorites is so important.

It is a two-step process. First, export your browser favorites to a file. In both Internet Explorer and Firefox, the Export and Import features can be found under the File menu. Once you have exported to a file, copy that file to the new PC and then import that file to your browser of choice on the new PC.

7. Install needed applications.

If your new PC is at work, chances are that all of the "necessary" applications are installed already. But for home PCs, there is still work to do. Everyone's idea of what applications should be installed is going to be a personal choice, but there are likely to be some selections common to us all. Here are some of the applications I have to install with each new PC:

- Office Suite, including e-mail client
- Money, QuickBooks, or some other money management application
- RSS Reader
- iTunes
- Graphics/Paint program beyond Paint for Windows
- VPN client (for connecting to the office)
- CD/DVD burning applications beyond what shipped with the PC
- HTML Editor
- Application developer IDE (often two—VS and Eclipse)

I'm sure you can think of some others. Of course there are always the entertainment applications like World of Warcraft, Call of Duty, and Civilization.

8. Set up e-mail and home page.

Now that you have your e-mail client and browser installed, it is time to configure them. Specifying the browser home page is an easy thing to do, but it is also quite necessary. The default home page for browsers is not where you want to go every time you fire it up. The e-mail client configuration will be dependent on the client application and the service provider. In Outlook, the configuration is under Tools | E-mail Accounts, which starts a wizard that will walk you through the process.

9. Install PowerToys.

One of the more important things you can do to enhance your new PC, especially if it is a Windows PC, is to install the Microsoft Windows XP PowerToys (http://techrepublic.com.com/5138-10877-5875848.html). These free applications can simplify your Windows PC life by making it easier to change default configurations, synchronize across computers, and manipulate files and photographs.

10. Save system and registry and back up.

Once you have your new PC set up the way you like it, take a few moments to back up your hard drive and save the system files and the registry. Taking these steps to establish a restore point now will create a new base configuration for your PC (http://techrepublic.com.com/5100-10877-5728564.html). This is a state you can return to if something goes wrong in the future. ❖

10+ things you should know when deploying Windows desktops from images

By Bill Detwiler

Properly configured and maintained system images can dramatically reduce desktop deployment and support times. Images also standardize systems, reducing surprises during support calls. Furthermore, third-party disk imaging products, such as Symantec Ghost or Altiris Client Management Suite, have significantly simplified the image creation and maintenance process. The following 10+ tips will help you create a reliable Windows system image and successfully deploy that image across your organization.

1. Create as few images as possible—one is best.

Having few, or a single, system images reduces the time required to build and maintain reliable images and simplifies the deployment process. Windows versions prior to XP often required a unique image for each desktop hardware configuration.

Windows XP and later versions allow you to install a single image across multiple hardware configurations providing the image meets a few conditions. First, the reference and destination computers must have identical Hardware Abstraction Layers (HALs) (http://support.microsoft.com/?id=309283). Second, the reference and destination machines must have the same Advanced Configuration and Power Interface (ACPI) support. Third, the reference and destination computers must have identical mass–storage controllers (IDE or SCSI). Fourth, you must have device drivers available for all Plug-and-Play devices on the destination computer. Lastly, the destination computer's hard drive must be at least the same size as the reference computer's hard disk. If the destination computer's hard drive is larger, the primary partition will not include the extra space. If the primary partition was formatted using NTFS, you can extend the primary partition using the ExtendOemPartition entry in the Sysprep.inf file.

2. Test and retest your image.

Unless your desktops have extremely similar hardware configurations, you should test your image on each type of machine you use. While it's not necessary for desktops to have exactly the same Plug-and-Play device configurations, they must support the same HAL and mass-storage device. It's particularly important to test the image on your desktops and laptops, if you plan to use the same image for both.

3. Use a slipstream CD to install Windows, relevent service packs, and updates.

When you install a Windows update or service pack, the installation process creates a backup of existing files that allows you to uninstall the update or service pack. This process works well on existing Windows machines with plenty of storage, but the uninstall files are unnecessary for and can significantly bloat your image. You want to keep your image as small and clean as possible.

Instead of installing Windows on the reference machine and then applying individual service packs, create a slipstream CD with all relevant updates and install from that CD. For information on creating a Windows XP slipstream CD, check out Greg Shultz's TechRepublic article, "Creating a quick Windows XP SP2 slipstream CD" at http://techrepublic.com.com/5100-10877_11-5630356.html.

4. Appropriately configure the self-healing properties for all Microsoft software.

If your image will include Microsoft applications, such as Office, you should properly configure each application's installation source. If an installation file becomes corrupt or the user wants to install new application features, the Windows Installer will look for the necessary files using the installation source path. If the application was installed from a CD, the source path would be the letter of the local installation drive. If the application was installed from a network CD image, the source path will likely be the network location.

It's often helpful for users to have an installation source path other than the default or multiple source paths: users may not have an installation CD; if one installation source is unavailable users will have a backup; having an installation source for each office or geographic region will reduce network traffic. After installing the application you can specify a new source path by editing the following registry key:

```
HKEY_LOCAL_MACHINE\SOFTWARE\Classes\Installer\Products\
  Product Code\SourceList\Net
```

Where *Product Code* is the application's unique product code. For example, the following registry key shows the product code for Microsoft Office 2003.

```
HKEY_LOCAL_MACHINE\SOFTWARE\Classes\Installer\Products\
  9040210900063D11C8EF10054038389C
```

5. Ensure the image includes all necessary site licenses and free software.

If your organization has site licenses for WinZip, a VPN client, SnagIt, or other utilities, put them on the image. Likewise, ensure that your image has commonly used freeware applications—Adobe Acrobat Reader, Microsoft's Visio Viewer, and the like. Having these applications on the image, means you don't have to install them later.

While WinZip may take only five minutes to install, consider installing it on 1,000 machines. That's a total of 5,000 minutes or slightly more than 83 hours. Even if you push these applications with a network installation package, you must still build the package, troubleshoot the failed installations, and take time away from your users. Put the utilities on the image and save yourself and your users time.

6. Create a clean, carefully planned Default User profile.

Keep in mind that your image's Default User profile will be copied to every imaged desktop in the organization. You should therefore be very thoughtful when creating this profile. Consider whether you want to use the Windows XP default Start menu or the Classic Start menu. How do you want the Programs menu to look? Do all the shortcuts work correctly? What shortcuts do you want on the Desktop?

To create the image's Default User profile, you should create a new user profile on the reference machine (named anything you want), configure the profile as you want, and then use it to replace the contents of the Default User profile folder—usually found at C:\Documents and Settings\Default User.

7. Defrag the reference computer before creating the image.

Once you've built and tested your reference machine's configuration, you should defragment the hard drive before actually creating the image. As you installed software on the reference machine, you likely fragmented the hard drive. Don't transfer this fragmentation to every destination machine you image and then require each user to defragment the hard drive as soon as the image process is complete. This simple trick will save you and your users time in the long run.

8. Learn and live Microsoft's System Preparation Tool (Sysprep).

Sysprep, available on the Windows XP CD, will prepare the reference computer to be imagined and create the Sysprep.inf answer—used during installation on the reference computer. This allows you to customize the image and installation process. For detailed directions on using Sysprep, check out Diana Huggins' TechRepublic Pro article "Using Sysprep to create a Windows XP image" (http://techrepublic.com.com/5100-6346-5838633.html) and Microsoft Knowledge Base (MSKB) article 302577, "How to use the Sysprep tool to automate successful deployment of Windows XP" (http://support.microsoft.com/default.aspx?scid=kb;en-us;302577).

9. Download the Windows XP Service Pack 2 Deployment Tools from Microsoft's Web site.

While these tools are available on the Windows XP CD, you should download the latest set of deploy tools, such as Windows XP Service Pack 2 Deployment Tools (http://www.microsoft.com/downloads/details.aspx?FamilyID=3e90dc91-ac56-4665-949b-beda3080e0f6&displayLang=en) from the Microsoft Web site. This file contains updated files and documentation helpful for imaging and deploying images across multiple computers.

10. Use third-party imaging software and deployment tools if applicable.

Third-party disk imaging products, such as Symantec Ghost or Altiris Client Management Suite, significantly simplify image creation and maintenance. They allow you to open and edit an image file without having to actually install the image on a reference machine and then recreate the image. This saves a significant amount of time when update your images. These third-party tools also have other benefits, such as allowing you to add startup scripts to the image.

11. Use PXE server.

The Preboot Execution Environment (PXE) protocol and services can be used to remotely boot a PC and initiate system software downloads. Most modern enterprise desktops should have PXE-complaint network interface cards (NICs). Using Microsoft's Remote Installation Services (RIS) or a third-party deployment application, such as Altiris Client Management Suite, and a PXE server, you can remotely image destination machines.

12. Regularly update the image.

As your organization buys new machines, you will undoubtedly need to update your image with appropriate OEM drivers. You will also want to include new Windows Service Packs and critical security updates. This doesn't mean you need to update your image each month when Microsoft releases a new patch. But you should update your image to reflect significant system changes, such as adopting a new service pack, acquiring a new site-licensed product, deploying a new office productivity suite, and so forth. ❖

10 things you can do when Windows XP won't boot

By Greg Shultz

When your computer hardware appears to power up okay, but the Windows XP operating system won't boot properly, you have to begin a troubleshooting expedition that includes getting into the operating system, determining the problem, and then fixing it. To help you get started on this expedition, here are 10 things you can do when Windows XP won't boot.

1. Use a Windows startup disk.

One of the first things you should reach for when troubleshooting a Windows XP boot problem is a Windows startup disk. This floppy disk can come in handy if the problem is being caused when either the startup record for the active partition or the files that the operating system uses to start Windows have become corrupted.

To create a Windows startup disk, insert a floppy disk into the drive of a similarly configured, working Windows XP system, launch My Computer, right-click the floppy disk icon, and select the Format command from the context menu. When you see the Format dialog box, leave all the default settings as they are and click the Start button. Once the format operation is complete, close the Format dialog box to return to My Computer, double-click the drive C icon to access the root directory, and copy the following three files to the floppy disk:

- Boot.ini
- NTLDR
- Ntdetect.com

After you create the Windows startup disk, insert it into the floppy drive on the afflicted system and press [Ctrl][Alt][Delete] to reboot the computer. When you boot from the Windows startup disk, the computer will bypass the active partition and boot files on the hard disk and attempt to start Windows XP normally.

2. Use Last Known Good Configuration.

You can also try to boot the operating system with the Last Known Good Configuration feature. This feature will allow you to undo any changes that caused problems in the CurrentControlSet registry key, which defines hardware and driver settings. The Last Known Good Configuration feature replaces the contents of the CurrentControlSet registry key with a backup copy that was last used to successfully start up the operating system.

To use the Last Known Good Configuration feature, first restart the computer by pressing [Ctrl][Alt][Delete]. When you see the message *Please select the operating system to start* or hear the single beep, press [F8] to display the Windows Advanced Options menu. Select the Last Known Good Configuration item from the menu and press [Enter].

Keep in mind that you get only one shot with the Last Known Good Configuration feature. In other words, if it fails to revive your Windows XP on the first attempt, the backup copy is also corrupt.

3. Use System Restore.

Another tool that might be helpful when Windows XP won't boot is System Restore. System Restore runs in the background as a service and continually monitors system-critical components for changes. When it detects an impending change, System Restore immediately makes backup copies, called restore points, of these critical components before the change occurs. In addition, System Restore is configured by default to create restore points every 24 hours.

To use System Restore, first restart the computer by pressing [Ctrl][Alt][Delete]. When you see the message *Please select the operating system to start* or hear the single beep, press [F8] to display the Windows Advanced Options menu. Now, select the Safe Mode item from the menu and press [Enter].

Once Windows XP boots into Safe mode, click the Start button, access the All Programs | Accessories | System Tools menu, and select System Restore. Because you're running in Safe mode, the only option on the opening screen of the System Restore wizard is Restore My Computer To An Earlier Time, and it's selected by default, so just click Next. Then, follow along with the wizard to select a restore point and begin the restoration procedure.

4. Use Recovery Console.

When a Windows XP boot problem is severe, you'll need to use a more drastic approach. The Windows XP CD is bootable and will provide you with access to a tool called Recovery Console.

To boot from the Windows XP CD, insert it into the CD-ROM drive on the problem system and press [Ctrl][Alt][Delete] to reboot the computer. Once the system begins booting from the CD, simply follow the prompts that will allow the loading of the basic files needed to run Setup. When you see the Welcome To Setup screen press R to start the Recovery Console.

You'll then see a Recovery Console menu. It displays the folder containing the operating system's files and prompts you to choose the operating system you want to log on to. Just press the menu number on the keyboard, and you'll be prompted to enter the Administrator's password. You'll then find yourself at the main Recovery Console prompt.

5. Fix a corrupt Boot.ini.

As the Windows XP operating system begins to load, the Ntldr program refers to the Boot.ini file to determine where the operating system files reside and which options to enable as the operating system continues to load. So if there's a problem rooted in the Boot.ini file, it can render Windows XP incapable of booting correctly.

If you suspect that Windows XP won't boot because Boot.ini has been corrupted, you can use the special Recovery Console version of the Bootcfg tool to fix it. Of course, you must first boot the system with the Windows XP CD and access the Recovery Console as described in #4.

To use the Bootcfg tool, from the Recovery Console command prompt, type

```
Bootcfg /parameter
```

Where */parameter* is one of the required parameters listed in the table below.

Parameter	Description
`/Add`	Scans the disk for all Windows installations and allows you to add any new ones to the Boot.ini file.
`/Scan`	Scans the disk for all Windows installations.
`/List`	Lists each entry in the Boot.ini file.
`/Default`	Sets the default operating system as the main boot entry.
`/Rebuild`	Completely re-creates the Boot.ini file. The user must confirm each step.
`/Redirect`	Allows the boot operation to be redirected to a specific port when using the Headless Administration feature. The Redirect parameter takes two parameters of its own: [Port Baudrate] | [UseBiosSettings].
`/Disableredirect`	Disables the redirection.

6. Fix a corrupt partition boot sector.

The partition boot sector is a small section of the hard disk partition that contains information about the operating system's file system (NTFS or FAT32), as well as a very small machine language program that is crucial in assisting the operating system as it loads.

If you suspect that Windows XP won't boot because the partition boot sector has been corrupted, you can use a special Recovery Console tool called Fixboot to fix it. Start by booting the system with the Windows XP CD and accessing the Recovery Console as described in #4.

To use the Fixboot tool, from the Recovery Console command prompt, type

```
Fixboot [drive]:
```

7. Fix a corrupt master boot record.

The master boot record occupies the first sector on the hard disk and is responsible for initiating the Windows boot procedure. The master boot record contains the partition table for the disk as well as a small program called the *master boot code*, which is responsible for locating the active, or bootable, partition in the partition table. Once this occurs, the partition boot sector takes over and begins loading Windows. If the master boot record is corrupt, the partition boot sector can't do its job and Windows won't boot.

If you suspect Windows XP won't boot because the master boot record has been corrupted, you can use the Recovery Console tool Fixmbr to fix it. First, boot the system with the Windows XP CD and access the Recovery Console as described in #4.

To use the Fixmbr tool, from the Recovery Console command prompt, type

```
Fixmbr [device_name]
```

Where `[device_name]` is the device pathname of the drive to which you want to write a new master boot record. For example, the device pathname format for a standard bootable drive C configuration would look like this:

```
\Device\HardDisk0
```

8. Disable automatic restart.

When Windows XP encounters a fatal error, the default setting for handling such an error is to automatically reboot the system. If the error occurs while Windows XP is booting, the operating system will become stuck in a reboot cycle—rebooting over and over instead of starting up normally. In that case, you'll need to disable the option for automatically restarting on system failure.

When Windows XP begins to boot up and you see the message *Please select the operating system to start* or hear the single beep, press [F8] to display the Windows Advanced Options menu. Then, select the Disable The Automatic Restart On System Failure item and press [Enter]. Now, Windows XP will hang up when it encounters the error, and with any luck, it will display a stop message you can use to diagnose the problem.

9. Restore from a backup.

If you can't seem to repair a Windows XP system that won't boot and you have a recent backup, you can restore the system from the backup media. The method you use to restore the system will depend on what backup utility you used, so you'll need to follow the utility's instructions on how to perform a restore operation.

10. Perform an in-place upgrade.

If you can't repair a Windows XP system that won't boot and you don't have a recent backup, you can perform an in-place upgrade. Doing so reinstalls the operating system into the same folder, just as if you were upgrading from one version of Windows to another. An in-place upgrade will usually solve most, if not all, Windows boot problems.

Performing a Windows XP in-place upgrade is pretty straightforward. To begin, insert the Windows XP CD into the drive, restart your system, and boot from the CD. Once the initial preparation is complete, you'll see the Windows XP Setup screen. Press [Enter] to launch the Windows XP Setup procedure. In a moment, you'll see the License Agreement page and will need to press [F8] to acknowledge that you agree. Setup will then search the hard disk looking for a previous installation of Windows XP. When it finds the previous installation, you'll see a second Windows XP Setup screen.

This screen will prompt you to press R to repair the selected installation or to press [Esc] to install a fresh copy of Windows XP. In this case, initiating a repair operation is synonymous with performing an in-place upgrade, so you'll need to press R. When you do so, Setup will examine the disk drives in the system. It will then begin performing the in-place upgrade.

Keep in mind that after you perform an in-place upgrade or repair installation, you must reinstall all updates to Windows. ❖

10 PowerToys that complete the Windows toolset and save you precious time

Compiled by Mark W. Kaelin

The Windows XP PowerToys are a set of applications and utilities you can download and install for free from Microsoft. They are not officially part of the operating system, but Microsoft makes them available as enhancements to the released product. In many cases, the functionality they provide is something that should have been available in Windows all along, but for some reason is not. As such, many of the Power Toys should be considered essential to the proper functioning of the OS. Here is a list of 10 of the more useful free utilities you can download at the Windows XP Power Toys site (http://www.microsoft.com/windowsxp/downloads/powertoys/xppowertoys.mspx).

Note

Keep in mind that while Microsoft ensures that the PowerToys for Windows XP work as described, it stops short of guaranteeing the package. Furthermore, the toys aren't officially supported by Microsoft, which means that Microsoft Technical Support won't answer questions on problems with the PowerToys.

1. Tweak UI

This utility allows you access to various user interface options and settings not available in the normal Windows XP control panel, like mouse and taskbar settings.

2. Clear Type Tuner

This utility helps you tune the shape and width of the fonts on your screen to better match your particular eye using ClearType Technology. This is a must for anyone with less than perfect vision.

3. Alt-Tab Replacement

For many power users the Alt-Tab keyboard shortcut for switching between running applications is a vital part of their interaction with Windows XP. Besides showing the icon of the application being switched to, this Alt-Tab Replacement Power Toy adds a thumbnail preview of what the window looks like, making the switch that much more intuitive.

4. Image Resizer

Whether you are dealing with digital photographs of your children's birthday party or screenshots for a million-dollar presentation, there will come a time when you will want to change the size of an image. This utility places that functionality in the right-click menu for any image file you can access through Windows Explorer.

5. SyncToy

The newest Windows XP PowerToy is the SyncToy (http://www.microsoft.com/windowsxp/using/digitalphotography/prophoto/synctoy.mspx), which was released in August 2005. This utility lets you synchronize two file folders on the same PC or different PCs across a network.

6. RAW Image Thumbnailer and Viewer

With this feature addition to Windows Explorer you can manipulate images in the RAW format (http://www.microsoft.com/windowsxp/using/digitalphotography/prophoto/raw.mspx) as easily as you can JPEG or GIF images. The RAW format is the default format produced by most digital cameras.

7. Open Command Window Here

Sometimes you just can't get around it—sometimes you need to use a command line to do a job and do it right. This little utility will open a command-line prompt in the selected directory rather than the root directory, which is the default.

8. Power Calculator

While the calculator app that ships with Windows XP is adequate for basic math calculations, you will often find yourself looking for some additional functionality. The Power Calculator provides those additional features including functions, graphing, precision settings, and basic, but useful, conversions.

9. Virtual Desktop Manager

Power users tend to have numerous applications running at the same time. During a major project for example, the number of applications running can be difficult to manage. With the Virtual Desktop Manager PowerToy you can create up to four separate virtual desktops, each with its own set of running applications. This powerful tool can help you manage your time and increase your overall efficiency.

10. HTML and CD Slide Show Wizard

This last tool is really two separate PowerToys that do the same thing, only in different places. These slide show wizards help you set up an image gallery as a basic slide show on either a CD-ROM or in HTML. This handy utility is good for automating simple presentations that don't need the extra features available in PowerPoint for example.

Installation

Installing the PowerToys for Windows XP is easy. Double-click the PowerToy-Setup.exe installation file, and the install wizard will begin the procedure. When you get to the Setup Type page, you can choose either the Complete or Custom setup options. ❖

10 things you should know about fighting spyware in Windows XP

By Greg Shultz

Today's cybercriminals are a crafty bunch, and they've mastered the art of infiltrating your computer and populating it with spyware—a broad category of malicious software programs installed on your computer without your knowledge or permission. Spyware is designed to operate in the background to perform such dubious tasks as gathering information about your computer usage and reporting back to a central database or diverting control of your computer to operations that benefit a cybercriminal's goals. Regardless of the nature of the spyware, it is definitely in your best interest to get rid of it as fast as you can. Here are 10 things you should know about fighting spyware in Windows XP.

1. Identify the presence of spyware.

Since spyware is designed to infiltrate your computer and clandestinely run in the background, how do you know when it is present? Even though spyware does its best to be sneaky, you can look for several telltale signs to identify the existence of spyware on your computer:

- Mysterious abundance of pop-up advertisements
- Internet Explorer's home and search pages suddenly change
- Internet Explorer contains uninvited components, such as toolbars
- Unknown icons appear on desktop, system tray, or toolbars
- Computer boots slower, runs sluggishly, or unexplainably crashes

2. Keep your operating system and software up to date.

All kinds of malicious applications are designed to seek out and take advantage of vulnerabilities in your operating system and software. So one important key to keeping spyware at bay is to proactively keep your Windows operating system and Microsoft software as up to date as possible:

- Upgrade Windows XP with SP2 (http://www.microsoft.com/windowsxp/sp2).
- Make sure that the Automatic Updates feature is enabled in Windows XP SP2's Security Center.
- Switch from Windows Update to Microsoft Update. (Connect to the Windows Update site (http://www.windowsupdate.com/) and click the Upgrade To Microsoft Update link).

3. Use a firewall.

A firewall can be either hardware or software that monitors your Internet connection and blocks unsolicited requests to gain access to your system. Even if you have a hardware firewall on your network, you should run a software firewall on your computer. Doubling your protection never hurts.

If you're running Windows XP SP2, the Windows Firewall is turned on by default. However, you can install and use any third-party firewall software you want. To learn more about using and configuring the Windows XP SP2 Windows Firewall, read the Microsoft article "Understanding Windows Firewall" (http://www.microsoft.com/windowsxp/using/security/internet/sp2_wfintro.mspx).

4. Scan your system with an anti-spyware program.

You should regularly use an anti-spyware program, which will scan for and remove spyware from your computer. Although a number of commercial anti-spyware scanning programs are available, you'll also find several good anti-spyware programs that are free to download and use:

- Spybot Search & Destroy (http://www.safer-networking.org/)
- Ad-Aware SE Personal Edition from Lavasoft (http://www.lavasoft.de/)
- Microsoft Windows AntiSpyware beta (http://www.microsoft.com/athome/security/spyware/software/default.mspx)

5. Know spyware when you see it.

After using an anti-spyware program to scan your system, you may end up viewing a report with a huge list of items reported as spyware. Some items are obviously spyware, such as something called ClickWatch, but other items might not be so easy to identify. Then you're left trying to decide whether to remove the item or leave it alone. When you're in doubt, here are a few ways to seek answers:

- Check you anti-spyware vendor's site; they often keep a database of spyware offenders and detailed information.
- Check the Spyware Guide site at http://www.spywareguide.com/.
- Check Computer Associate's Spyware Encyclopedia at http://www3.ca.com/securityadvisor/pest/search.aspx.
- Just go to http://www.google.com/ and Google the name of the item and see what turns up.

6. Use a real-time antispyware scanner.

If you can't seem to avoid spyware sources or your computer is used by young surfers who may not understand the threat posed by spyware, you should consider using an antispyware program with a real-time monitoring component that runs in the background, looking for and blocking spyware as you surf the Internet. For example, Spybot Search & Destroy provides a real-time monitoring component called TeaTimer. The free version of Ad-Aware doesn't contain a real-time monitoring component—you have to purchase one of the Ad-Aware versions that contains the Ad-Watch real-time monitoring component.

7. Keep Internet Explorer's Internet zone set to Medium.

Spyware primarily infiltrates your system via Web sites containing hidden traps that ambush your computer before you have a chance to figure out what's going on. To protect your computer from such unauthorized access, Internet Explorer provides a range of Security settings that control how much information you'll automatically accept from a Web site. When you install SP2, the setup procedure sets the Internet zone to Medium, which is the recommended level. A Medium security setting offers just enough access to make Web browsing enjoyable, yet safe.

It's easy to change the Security settings, and someone may inadvertently (or intentionally) lower the level, thus opening the door to spyware. As a result, it's a good idea to keep tabs on Internet Explorer's Security settings for the Internet zone:

1. From within Internet Explorer, pull down the Tools menu and select Internet Options.
2. In the Internet Options dialog box, choose the Security tab.
3. Select the Internet zone and check the Security Level setting.
4. If it's not set to Medium, click the Default Level button.

For more information on Internet Explorer's Security settings, see the Microsoft article "Working with Internet Explorer 6 Security Settings" (http://www.microsoft.com/windows/ie/using/howto/security/settings.mspx).

8. Use Microsoft's online Malicious Software Removal Tool.

If you suspect that your system has been compromised by some form of spyware, chances are good that other malicious software snuck in at the same time. In that case, you may want to use Microsoft's online Malicious Software Removal Tool to check for other anomalies. (Microsoft updates this tool with new signatures on the second Tuesday of each month.)

1. Use Internet Explorer to connect to the Malicious Software Removal Tool page at http://www.microsoft.com/security/malwareremove/default.mspx.
2. In the Scan And Clean Your PC panel, click the Check My PC For Infection button.

3. When you see the Microsoft End-User License Agreement dialog box, select the I Agree option and click Continue.
4. If Internet Explorer prompts you to install the ActiveX control, allow the installation and then click the Check My PC For Infection button again.
5. When prompted to install the Malicious Software Removal Tool, click the Install button.
6. When the scan is complete, review the report displayed on the page.

9. Use the Pop-Up Blocker.

Pop-up windows containing innocuous advertisements or goofy messages are often the calling card of some devious spyware program. By default, SP2 installs and enables Internet Explorer's Pop-up Blocker with the default Filter level setting of Medium. However, this setting will often block legitimate pop-ups that users need to see. As a result, many people decide that the inconvenience is more annoying than the potential risk and turn off Pop-up Blocker. It's easy to do: Tools | Pop-up Blocker | Turn Off Pop-up Blocker.

However, the ability to display a pop-up is often all the spyware needs to infiltrate a system. So instead of turning off the Pop-up Blocker, you should use the Exceptions feature to allow pop-ups from those Web sites you trust:

1. Choose Tools | Pop-up Blocker | Pop-up Blocker Settings.
2. Type the address of the Web site in the appropriate text box and click the Add button.
3. Make sure that the Filter Level setting is set to Medium.
4. Click the Close button.

10. Close pop-ups properly.

If you do happen to encounter a pop-up window, don't click any button inside the window no matter what it says. A lot of spyware will try to trick you into allowing it into your system by prompting you to click an innocent-looking OK or Cancel button in a window designed to look like a dialog box. Never do that! Always use the red Close button in the upper-right corner of the window. ❖

10 things you can do to optimize Virtual PC

By Steven S. Warren

Microsoft Virtual PC 2004 is Microsoft's flagship workstation software virtualization product. After installing Virtual PC and loading your environment, follow these 10 steps for optimal performance.

1. Store your virtual image on a separate drive.

Your virtual image has an extension with the name of *.vhd. When creating virtual disks, you want to store them on a separate drive. You take a performance hit by keeping your virtual disks on the same drive as your operating system. If you run virtual machines on your laptop, you may get increased performance by running your virtual machines off a USB 2.0 drive.

2. Stay on top of service packs and VM additions.

Keep your computer up to date on the latest service packs, including any service packs with Virtual PC. If you have Virtual PC loaded currently, make sure you are running Service Pack 1 for Virtual PC and load the VM additions on all of your previous virtual machines.

3. Ensure sufficient memory.

It is important for you to have plenty of memory to run virtual machines concurrently. At a minimum, to run one or two virtual machines, you would need 512. We recommend at least 1 GB if not 2 GB.

4. Defragment the computer.

Make sure you defrag both your computer and virtual disk to keep your system running optimally.

5. Run Virtual PC at maximum speed.

Go into the Virtual PC options and make sure your virtual machines are running at maximum speed.

6. Use fixed size instead of dynamic.

Using a fixed-size disk, if possible, will really increase performance. Remember to size it properly.

7. Zero the free space on your virtual disk.

Run your virtual machine as local administrator and mount the Virtual Disk Precompactor.iso from \Program Files\Microsoft Virtual PC\Virtual Machine Additions. Follow the prompts to precompact and remember to clear the temp directory and event logs prior to rebooting.

8. Compress the virtual hard disk.

Edit the settings of the virtual disk and choose Compact It.

9. Eliminate the page file.

You can get better performance from your virtual machines and save disk space by eliminating the page file.

10. Experiment.

By experimenting, you can really optimize your virtual machines. For example, deleting the dllcach folder saves you 400 MB. Emptying the i386 folder and $NTSERVICEPACKUNINSTALL$ folder saves you roughly 250 MB. Delete files you don't need. Examples include help files, sounds, pictures, logs, cache, and backups. Anything that can decrease the size of your virtual machine and that will not break the operating system is fair game. Other examples include deleting Music, removing wallpaper, and turning off system restore. ❖

10 things you should know about working with the Windows Registry

By Greg Shultz

The Windows registry is essentially a database of all the configuration settings in the Windows operating system. It contains profiles for every user who has an account on the local system, information about all internal and external hardware connected to the computer, information about all the applications installed in the operating system, and the details about every configuration setting made throughout the operating system.

Because the Windows registry is like the brain of the operating system, you need to be extremely careful anytime you make a change to it. To help you work effectively with the registry and avoid the potentially dire consequences of an editing mistake, we've put together this list of things you should know when working with the Windows registry.

1. The lay of the registry

Before you begin any journey, a map is a helpful tool. Not only will it help you plan your route, but it will also help you to get a feel for the environment you're about to encounter. The same thing can be said for the Windows registry.

The Windows registry is made up of five main sections, called *keys*, each containing specific types of information about the operating system. Microsoft also uses the term *hives* to refer to these five sections. Regardless of which name you use, each section resembles a nested folder structure containing files of settings called *values*. These are the five main keys in the Windows registry:

- HKEY_CLASSES_ROOT—This key represents information about file types.
- HKEY_CURRENT_USER—This key contains copies of data stored in HKEY_USERS about the user who is currently logged on.
- HKEY_LOCAL_MACHINE—This key represents information about all the hardware and software installed on the computer.
- HKEY_USERS—This key represents information about all the users who have accounts on the system.
- HKEY_CURRENT_CONFIG—This key essentially contains copies of the information from all the other root keys that pertain to the currently running session.

2. Backing up the registry

Before you ever make any changes to the registry, you should make a backup copy of it. That way, should you make a critical mistake, you have a way to return the system to a viable state. Here are several methods you can use to back up the registry:

- Use Windows XP's Backup Utility and select System State.
- Create a restore point.
- Launch the Registry Editor, select the key you plan to edit, pull down the File menu, and choose the Export command.

3. The Registry Editor

To manually view and modify the registry, you can use the Registry Editor. You launch the Registry Editor by accessing the Run dialog box (Start | Run), typing Regedit in the Open text box, and clicking OK. When using the Registry Editor, be careful that you don't change a key or value not related to the change you want to make.

4. Using REG files

If the registry edit you want to make is a fairly common one and you don't want to manually edit the registry with the Registry Editor, perform a Google search for a REG file that will perform the edit for you. (Be careful that the site you choose is a reputable one.) A REG file is a special text file, exported from the Registry Editor, that contains the commands to perform the registry edit. You simply double-click the REG file, and it will automatically import the edit into your registry.

5. Using a GUI tool

Since the registry is the main repository for the majority of the configuration settings in the operating system, chances are good that there is a GUI tool you can use to make your registry changes. Of course, just about all the tools in the Control Panel make changes to the registry. Another native operating system tool you can use to make registry changes is the Group Policy editor. (Just type *Gpedit.msc* in the Run dialog box.) To make changes to the registry that are not found in native tools, you can download the Microsoft TweakUI PowerToy at http://www.microsoft.com/windowsxp/downloads/powertoys/xppowertoys.mspx.

6. Searching the registry

If you know the name of the subkey or value you want to edit in the registry but you don't know exactly where it's located, keep in mind that the Registry Editor has a nice little Find tool. To access it from within the Registry Editor, just press [Ctrl]F. When you see the Find dialog box, type the name of the subkey or value you want to search for in the text box and then select or clear any of the check boxes in the Look At panel (Keys, Values, or Data) to better target your search.

7. Taking advantage of Favorites

If you find yourself regularly editing the registry from within the Registry Editor, you can use the Registry Editor's Favorites menu to save yourself time tracking down a deeply nested subkey you edited previously. As with Internet Explorer, the Registry Editor's Favorites menu allows you to bookmark locations—but in this case, those locations are in the registry. When you make a registry change you'll want to return to at a later date, just pull down the Favorites menu and select the Add To Favorites command. Then, you can use the Favorites menu to quickly return to that exact subkey whenever you need to.

8. Working around the Registry Editor's LastKey feature

The Registry Editor comes with a feature called LastKey. This feature saves the path to the key that's open when you close the Registry Editor. The next time you launch the Registry Editor, it automatically displays that key. Although this feature is designed to make it easier for you to make changes to a specific key without having to drill down through the registry tree each time, it can be annoying when you need to edit a different key. You're forced to close all the open branches before you can drill down to the new key.

To work around this feature when it's inconvenient, you can use the RegEd Launcher, which is available as a free TechRepublic download (http://techrepublic.com.com/5100-6346_11-5030730.html). When you run the RegEd Launcher, it displays a dialog box that asks you whether you want to open the Registry Editor at the last edited key or start a new editing session.

9. Cleaning the registry

Over time, the registry can become bloated with orphaned or corrupt keys and values, yet still function. However, this bloat can make the registry inefficient and slow. Microsoft used to provide a tool called RegClean that was specifically designed to analyze the registry and remove orphaned and corrupt keys and values. Unfortunately, the tool was never updated to run with Windows XP. However, there are many commercial and shareware registry cleaners out there that perform admirably. Here are a few to investigate:

- Registry Clean Pro http://www.registry-clean.com/
- Registry Mechanic http://www.pctools.com/
- TweakNow RegCleaner http://www.tweaknow.com/

10. Monitoring registry activity

When you install a new application, the installation procedure can make a multitude of changes to the registry—all behind the scenes. If you want to keep track of how the registry is altered, you need to investigate RegMon, a freeware utility from Systems Internals. RegMon is designed to run in the background and track registry I/O operations. It will then provide a report on the status of those operations, which can come in handy should you ever have to troubleshoot registry problems that you think are related to the application. ❖

10 things you should know about device driver rollback in Windows XP

By Brien M. Posey

1. Device driver rollback allows you to recover from the installation of an invalid, incorrect, or corrupt device driver.

Invalid, incorrect, or corrupt device drivers can cause lots of different problems. If such drivers are installed, they can render a system unbootable or trigger the Blue Screen of Death shortly after the system boots. In less extreme cases, they can cause the designated device and possibly other devices to fail.

2. The device driver rollback option is available through the Device Manager.

You can access the rollback option for a device driver by opening the Windows XP Control Panel and clicking the Performance And Maintenance link, followed by the System Link. Doing so will cause Windows to display the System Properties sheet. To access the Device Manager, go to the properties sheet's Hardware tab and click the Device Manager button.

The Device Manager is arranged by device in a hierarchical manner. Navigate through the console tree to the device that you need to roll the driver back for. Right-click on the device and select the Properties command from the resulting shortcut menu. You will now see the device's properties sheet. Select the Driver tab and click the Roll Back Driver button. If Windows has knowledge of a previous device driver, the rollback will now occur. If there was no previous version, you'll see an error message.

3. You can use a shortcut to access the Device Manager.

As you can see above, several steps are involved in getting to the point where you can roll back a device driver. Luckily, there's a shortcut. Just enter **DEVMGMT .MSC** at the Run prompt to go directly to the Device Manager.

4. If the system is unbootable, you can usually fix the problem through Safe Mode.

Safe Mode's job is to load the Windows GUI while running a minimal device driver set. In almost every case, if a driver renders the system unbootable, you can still boot the machine into Safe Mode (press the [F8] key during the earliest stages of the boot process).

5. If you can't fix the problem through Safe Mode, try using the Last Known Good Configuration.

In extreme cases, you may not be able to boot the machine into Safe Mode. In that event, you should try to boot using the Last Known Good Configuration option (also accessible by pressing [F8] during the earliest stages of the boot process). Using the Last Known Good Configuration option returns the system to the state that it was in (at least with respect to device drivers) the last time the boot process completed successfully. But if the device driver problem manifests itself after the login process, you won't be able to use the Last Known Good Configuration option to fix it.

6. If rolling back a device driver doesn't solve your problem, System Restore might be a better option.

There are times when rolling back a device driver may not fix the problem. If the system is bootable and rolling back the device driver isn't helping you, you may be able to correct the problem using System Restore. The System Restore feature takes snapshots of the operating system at various times and prior to potentially catastrophic events, such as device driver installations.

To access System Restore, select the All Programs | Accessories | System Tools | System Restore options from Windows Start menu. System Restore allows you to restore your system's settings from an earlier time.

7. The Device Driver Rollback feature can't be used to uninstall a device driver.

Earlier, you saw that if no previous version of a device driver was available, you would get an error message if you attempted a rollback. This means you can't use the device driver rollback feature as an uninstall utility. If you need to uninstall a device driver, click the Uninstall button.

8. You can't roll back all the drivers for a multifunction device simultaneously.

Some hardware devices, such as modems and sound cards, are broken down into multiple logical devices. For example, you can see several drivers listed under Sound, Video And Game Controllers. However, most of these drivers are for the same physical device. In situations in which multiple drivers apply to a single device, each of the individual drivers must be rolled back separately. There is no device-level rollback.

9. You can't roll back printer drivers.

There are a couple of reasons why you can't roll back printer drivers. For one thing, printers aren't listed within Device Manager. But the main reason is that printer drivers tend to be a lot more complex than other device drivers. A typical device driver is usually nothing more than an INF file, although there may be an associated DLL file. Printer drivers, on the other hand, can be huge. For example, I downloaded a new driver for my HP 7310 XI yesterday, and it was more than 200 MB in size.

10. You can't roll back more than one device driver version.

You can't roll back multiple driver versions. Windows caches only the previous driver version, not every driver version that was ever installed. If you need to revert to a much earlier driver version, your best option is to use System Restore. If you do use System Restore, remember that other aspects of your operating system may also be reverted back to earlier versions. ❖

10 things you should know about Automated System Recovery

By Brien M. Posey

1. Automated System Recovery can be a huge time saver.

If the system drive on your server fails, you would normally have to replace the drive and then manually install Windows and your backup software (if you are using third-party software) before you could even think about performing a system restore. With Automated System Recovery (ASR), you can restore Windows from a special backup rather than install it manually.

2. Automated System Recovery is supported only in Windows XP and Windows Server 2003.

ASR was first introduced in Windows XP. You can use it to restore a machine that's running Windows XP or Windows Server 2003, but not earlier versions of Windows.

3. You must perform a special Automated System Recovery backup.

You can't perform an automated system recovery using a normal backup. If you want to take advantage of ASR, you'll have to create an Automated System Recovery Backup. This is a special two-part backup that consists of the backup itself and a supplemental floppy disk that contains information regarding how Windows should restore the backup. When you launch NTBACKUP, the Welcome screen contains an Automated System Recovery Wizard option. You'll use this option to create an Automated System Recovery Backup.

4. Applications will not be restored as a part of an Automated System Recovery.

ASR does not perform a full, bare metal restore. Its job is just to return the Windows operating system to a functional state. An ASR backup is not a suitable replacement for your regular backup.

5. Automated System Recovery will format the system drive as a part of the restore operation .

To perform an automated system recovery, you must boot your computer from the Windows installation CD and then choose the Automated System Recovery option when prompted. As with a clean Windows installation, ASR will format the system drive as a part of the recovery process. Normally, this shouldn't be a problem, since ASR is intended for use after a hard disk failure. However, if your system drive contains data you want to salvage, running ASR is a bad idea.

6. The Automated System Recovery floppy disk is needed for the restore procedure.

When you perform an ASR backup, the process will create a supplemental floppy disk. The restore procedure requires you to have this floppy disk available. Since most computers today ship without floppy drives, you may also want to keep a spare floppy drive on hand in case you ever need to perform an automated system recovery.

7. If you have lost or damaged the Automated System Recovery floppy disk, you can create another one.

Although the supplemental floppy disk is required for an automated system restore, you are not up the creek if you should happen to lose or damage it. You can make a replacement disk on another machine. The catch is that your ASR backup must be accessible from the machine you're using to create the replacement disk.

To create the replacement disk, take the server's backup tape to another machine and restore the ASR.SIF and ASRPNP.SIF files to a floppy disk. These files are located in the \Windows\repair folder.

8. When an Automated System Recovery completes, you must update Windows.

When the ASR process completes, Windows will exist in the state it was in when you made the ASR backup (minus your applications and data). You will therefore have to restore a normal backup to get your applications and data back. However, depending on which applications you're running, simply restoring a backup at this point could cause some major problems that would result in your having to start the restore operation over from scratch. To avoid these potential problems, I recommend using Windows Update to bring the Windows operating system up to the same patch level that was in place when your most recent backup was made.

9. You may have to manually install some applications.

You may find that you have to manually install some applications prior to restoring your applications and data. One example of this is your backup software. If you use third-party backup software, you'll usually have to install your backup application before you will be able to restore your backup.

Another example is Exchange Server. The NTBACKUP program does not support the backup and restore of Exchange Server databases by default. NTBACKUP is extended to support Exchange only after Exchange is installed. Therefore, if Exchange databases are part of the data you plan on restoring, you may have to manually install Exchange before restoring your backup. If you find yourself in this situation, remember to install the most recent Exchange Service Pack as well before attempting a restore.

10. Don't depend on USB floppy drives.

As I mentioned earlier, a floppy drive is required for an Automated System Recovery. I've known some people who keep a USB-based floppy drive on hand in case of just such an emergency. However, ASR runs as a part of the Windows Setup process. During this process, Windows has a limited driver set and in most cases it won't recognize a USB floppy drive. ❖

10 things you should know about Windows XP's System Restore tool

By Greg Shultz

Windows XP's System Restore lets you restore your computer to a previous time if a problem occurs. To accomplish this feat, System Restore continuously monitors your system looking for significant changes to the operating system, such as an application or driver installation procedure, and automatically creating a restore point when it detects an impending change. System Restore will also create restore points every 24 hours. Restore points are essentially snapshots of your system state, which comprises crucial system files including certain parts of the registry. System Restore maintains multiple restore points, which gives you the choice of restoring your computer to any number of previously saved states. Here are 10 things you should know about getting the most from Windows XP's System Restore tool.

1. Data files and System Restore

Because System Restore is described as a tool that allows you to restore your computer to a *previous time*, many people mistakenly assume that they will lose any data files they've created since the restore point was created. However, System Restore doesn't monitor or save the contents of the My Documents folder; any files that use common data filename extensions, such as .doc or .xls; e-mail message stores; browsing history; or even password files. Those files will remain intact when you restore your system.

However, keep in mind that the Desktop is not a protected folder, and any files that exist there could be lost during a restore operation. So before you perform a restore operation, you should move any crucial files you have saved on the Desktop to the My Documents folder.

2. Undoing a restore operation

If you perform a restore operation and then determine that the problem still exists, you can undo the operation. To do so, you must immediately run System Restore. When you see the Welcome To System Restore screen, select the Undo My Last Restoration option and click Next. On the Confirm Restoration Undo screen, click Next. System Restore will restore the previous system state and restart the computer. When the system restarts and you log on, you'll see System Restore's Undo Complete screen, which lets you know the operation was successful.

If you perform a restore operation and then determine that you selected the wrong restore point date, simply run System Restore again and select the restore point date you wanted.

If you perform a successful restore operation and discover that your computer won't boot Windows normally, you can still undo the restore operation. First, boot the system into Safe Mode. After you log on, a Warning dialog box will appear, allowing you to launch System Restore and select the Undo My Last Restoration option.

If the restore operations fails, the Restoration Was Unsuccessful screen will appear, and your computer will automatically return to the same state it was in when you activated the restore operation. In other words, no changes will be made to your computer.

3. Running System Restore from a command prompt

If your computer won't boot Windows normally and won't boot into the Safe Mode GUI, you can still access System Restore. Start by booting the system using the Safe Mode With Command Prompt option. After you log on, type the following command line at the command prompt:

```
%systemroot%\system32\restore\rstrui.exe
```

Press [Enter], and System Restore will run as it normally does. You can follow the steps in the wizard to perform a restore operation.

4. Purging restore points

System Restore by default claims a maximum of 12 percent of the available hard disk space to save the restore points. (The amount of storage space will depend on the size of your hard disk.) Once the 12-percent mark is reached, System Restore will purge the oldest restore points in its database to make room for new ones. However, there may be situations where you need or want to purge restore points to free up disk space. Fortunately, the Disk Cleanup utility will allow you to delete all but the most recent restore point.

You can launch Disk Cleanup from the Start | All Programs | Accessories | System Tools menu. Once Disk Cleanup is up and running, select the More Options tab and click the Cleanup button in the System Restore panel. You'll then be prompted to confirm the delete operation.

5. Reining in System Restore's disk space usage

To perform its operations, System Restore requires at least 200 MB of available hard disk space. However, if more disk space is available, System Restore will claim up to 12 percent of it to save the restore points. Although System Restore can use that full 12 percent if it's available, this chunk of disk space is not reserved. System Restore will yield disk space back to the system if it's needed. Furthermore, restore points more than 90 days old are automatically purged by default.

If you want to see how much hard disk space System Restore has potentially set aside on your system, press [Windows][Break] to bring up the System Properties dialog box and then choose the System Restore tab. Next, select your hard disk from the Available Drive list and click the Settings button. When the Drive Settings dialog box appears, you'll see a number in the Disk Space Usage panel that represents the amount of space in MB that System Restore is using to amass restore points.

For example, on a system with an 80GB hard disk, System Restore's 12 percent amounts to nearly 9 GB. If you feel that System Restore has the potential to take up too much disk space, move the slider to the left to specify a more reasonable amount of hard disk space for System Restore to store its multiple restore points.

6. Manually creating a restore point

System Restore will automatically create restore points, but you can manually create one anytime you want. To do so, launch System Restore and then follow along with the wizard. If you want to save yourself a few steps, you can simplify the launching process by copying the System Restore shortcut from the Start | All Programs | Accessories | System Tools menu to the Desktop.

7. Bypassing the System Restore Wizard

If you want to be able to manually create a restore point without having to go through the wizard, you can create a simple two-line VBScript file that uses WMI (Windows Management Instrumentation) to instantly create a restore point. Just launch Notepad and type these two lines:

```
Set IRP = getobject("winmgmts:\\.\root\default:Systemrestore")

MYRP = IRP.createrestorepoint ("My Restore Point", 0, 100)
```

Then, save the file as MyRestorePoint.vbs. Now, you can easily create a restore point by double-clicking the script's icon. When you do, System Restore will run in the background without displaying its interface and will create a restore point called *My Restore Point.*

8. Steps to avoid restoring viruses

If you know that your system is infected by a virus, you should temporarily turn off System Restore. Otherwise, the virus could be saved along with other system files in a restore point and reintroduced to your system during a restore operation at a later date.

To turn off System Restore, press [Windows][Break] to bring up the System Properties dialog box. Then, choose the System Restore tab, select the Turn Off System Restore check box, and click OK. As soon as you do, you'll see a confirmation dialog box warning you that turning off System Restore will delete all existing restore points. Click Yes to continue.

You can now use your antivirus software to clean up your system. When the virus has been eradicated, access the System Restore tab again and clear the Turn Off System Restore check box. Click OK to re-enable System Restore.

9. Disabling System Restore for data drives

If you have additional hard disks connected to your computer, System Restore will automatically add them to its list of monitored drives. If these additional drives just store data or data backups, there's no reason to have System Restore monitor them.

To disable System Restore for data drives, press [Windows][Break] to bring up the System Properties dialog box. Then, choose the System Restore tab. Next, select your hard disk from the Available Drive list and click the Settings button. When the Drive Settings dialog box appears, select the Turn Off System Restore On This Drive check box and click OK. You'll see a confirmation dialog box warning that by turning off System Restore on this drive, you won't be able to track or undo harmful changes on it. Click Yes to continue. Then, click OK to close the System Properties dialog box.

10. Determining the actual amount of space System Restore is using

You can easily determine how much disk space System Restore can potentially use, but you may also want to determine how much disk space System Restore is actually using. If you're running Windows XP Professional and the hard disk is using NTFS, you can find out.

You'll begin by making a few configuration changes from an Administrator account that will allow you to investigate the hidden and protected folder called System Volume Information, located in the root directory of your hard disk. Keep in mind that this information is meant only for investigative purposes. Making any changes to the files in the System Volume Information folder will disrupt or otherwise damage System Restore's ability to do its job.

From within Windows Explorer, access the View tab of the Folder Options dialog box. Then, select the Show Hidden Files And Folders option, deselect the Hide Protected Operating System Files check box, and click Yes in the Warning dialog box. (If the system is in a workgroup, you'll need to deselect the Use Simple File Sharing check box as well.) Click OK to close the Folder Options dialog box.

Now, access the root directory of the hard disk, right-click on the System Volume Information folder, select Properties, and access the Security tab. Then, click the Add button, enter your user account name in the Select Users Or Groups dialog box, and click OK twice to close both dialog boxes.

At this point, you can open the System Volume Information folder, right-click on the restore folder, and select Properties. Once Windows XP finishes tallying, check the Size On Disk value to see the exact amount of space System Restore is using for restore points. To ensure the security of the restore point files, you should remove your user account from the System Volume Information folder once you finish your investigation. ❖

Notes:

2 Applications

10 things you can do to become an Outlook Web Access (OWA) power user

By Thomas W. Shinder, MCSE, MVP

Outlook Web Access (OWA) makes it possible for users with Exchange accounts to manage their e-mail from almost any computer that has a Web browser. The interface is similar to the Outlook client, so the learning curve is low for performing basic e-mail tasks. However, you can make your OWA experience even better. Here are 10 tips for becoming an OWA power user.

1. Use an = sign before an e-mail alias.

When you enter an e-mail alias into the To text box for a new e-mail message, you'll often be confronted with a dialog box asking what user you want to send the message to. For example, if you enter tshin, you'll be asked if you want to send the message to tshin or tshinder or tshindler or tshinmmer. You know that tshin is the alias you want, so why do you need to choose from the list? You don't! Just enter =tshin in the To text box and you won't see the dialog box asking which user you want to send the message to.

2. Use OWA hotkeys.

You can click your way through the OWA interface, but if you frequently use OWA when on the road or at your home office, there's a faster way—OWA hotkeys. Some of our favorites are:

- [Alt]S: Sends a message
- [Ctrl]S: Saves a message
- [Ctrl]D: Deletes a message
- [F7]: Checks the spelling of a message
- [Ctrl]R: Replies to a message
- [Ctrl]U: Marks the message as unread
- [Ctrl]K: Checks the name in the To: field

There are many more hotkeys. Click the Help entry in the OWA interface and choose Accessibility in the left pane of the console. You'll see a link to Keyboard Shortcuts.

3. Use column headers to quickly find messages.

Column headers in Outlook 2003 make it easy to quickly sort messages by Date, From, or Subject. You can do the same thing with OWA. Just click one of the column headers in the OWA interface and it will sort the messages, either from low to high or high to low. Click the column header again and it will switch directions, from high to low or low to high, depending on how the column was previously sorted.

4. Use built-in searching on column header sorting.

Although the column sorting is useful, you can take it to the next level by searching within a sorted column. For example, suppose you sorted your messages using the From header. Now you want to find all messages from Jim Harrison. Instead of scrolling through the list of names in the list of e-mail messages, you can use the built-in search function and drill down to the specific user.

Try this: In the OWA interface, click the From column header. Now type the first few letters in the sender name. For this example, we'll type Jim. The display changes focus to the messages that have Jim in the beginning of the From field. Make sure you don't hesitate when typing the characters; if you do, you might find you get inconsistent results.

5. Multiselect contiguous or noncontiguous days in the OWA Calendar.

The full Outlook 2003 client lets you see the day view for the entire work week. When using OWA, you can see a single day in full-day view. Your only other options are full week and month view. This can be a real bummer when you want to see what's happening in full-day view for multiple days.

The good news is that you're not limited to a single day. Click the Calendar link and then click 1 in the icon bar. Select a day in the month calendar in the right pane of the browser and then hold down the [Ctrl] key. Click on any other days you like—contiguous or noncontiguous—while the [Ctrl] key is held down. Let go of the [Ctrl] key and you'll see multiple days in day view. If you want to return to single day view, just click on that date in the calendar in the right pane of the console.

6. Speed up OWA connections over slow lines with basic OWA.

There are times when you just can't get a fast Internet connection. It often happens when you visit family members who aren't fully connected and have only dial-up connections. If you've ever tried to use OWA over a dial-up connection, you know it's not a satisfying experience. The solution for OWA access when you have a slow connection is to use the basic interface when logging on to your mailbox. The basic interface is quite a bit different from the full OWA experience, and it's not as fully functional. But you'll find it workable, and you'll be able to get to your e-mail much more quickly than when using the full OWA experience on a dial-up connection.

7. Get an Agenda view using a secret URL.

The full Outlook 2003 client provides a nifty Outlook Today view that allows you to see all your meeting and scheduled events for the day. I typically configure Outlook 2003 to open this page by default so that I can do a quick check on the day's events. The same functionality isn't included with OWA, so you have to go to the Calendar and check your day view to get something similar.

At least, that's the case if you don't use the secret URL that provides a daily Agenda. The URL is https://<servername>/exchange/<alias>/calendar/?cmd=contents&part=1 (or http: if you're not using secure connections). This feature was designed to work with SharePoint, but you don't need SharePoint to get this view. Just create a shortcut on your desktop with this URL and you'll be able to quickly get a rundown of your week's events.

8. Double-click to create a new meeting.

The full Outlook client allows you to create a new meeting at a specific time of day by double-clicking in the Calendar on the date and time you want the meeting to take place. Guess what? You can do the same thing in OWA. Just open the Calendar in OWA, enter the day view, and double-click on the time you want to schedule an event in your calendar. The new Appointment window opens and includes the start time on which you double-clicked.

9. Automatically include your signature in new messages.

Most of us who use the full Outlook client have a standard signature we want appended to our e-mail messages. You can do the same thing with the OWA client. While in the OWA interface, click the Options link in the left pane of the window to open the Options page. Select the Automatically Include My Signature On Outgoing Messages check box and then click Edit Signature. Enter your OWA signature in the text box and click OK. Unfortunately, the OWA signature feature can't pick up the signature you use in your full Outlook client.

10. Check spelling on each new message

Although it might not seem to be the case these days, spelling is still important—especially when writing messages to colleagues and business partners. Most of us can use all the help we can get when it comes to spelling, so why not let OWA give us a hand? While in the OWA interface, click the Options link in the left pane of the window to open the Options page. In the Spelling Options section, select the Always Check Spelling Before Sending check box. Click the Save And Close button in the OWA icon bar and you're good to go. ❖

10 things you should know about Google's Gmail service

By Mark W. Kaelin

Google continues to make its case as the only Web destination you ever need—much to the delight of its investors. One of the more useful Google offerings is the Gmail Web-based e-mailing application. Although technically still in beta, Gmail is in fact a very useful and feature-rich mostly complete application. However, not all the features that can be found in Gmail are readily apparent. The 10 things listed in this article will draw out some of the hidden features and make this Web-based e-mail client event more appealing.

1. Labels

When it comes to organizing your Gmail inbox, there is perhaps no better mechanism than the label feature. You can label any e-mail with a keyword or keywords of your own choosing. From that point on, that e-mail will be identified by its label(s) and, most importantly, can be searched and listed according to that label. Using this feature, you can basically index or tag your e-mail for later retrieval; only you get to decide what that system for retrieval looks like.

Creating and assigning labels can be accomplished under the More Actions dropdown box.

2. Conversations

A set of e-mails associated by a common label is known as a conversation. Certain actions, such as moving to a different folder, can be accomplished in a single pass on the entire conversation. This can save a tremendous amount of time if your conversation is a lengthy one. One caveat, don't add an e-mail to a conversation unless it is really an integral part of that thread, because any changes made to a conversation will be made across the board.

3. Searching multiple labels

The feature that separates Google's Gmail Web-based e-mail service from everyone else's is the searching capability—something that Google does very well obviously. Besides the typical keyword search, where you type in a word or phrase, click the Search button, and wade through the corresponding results, you can perform more advanced searches.

Advanced searches rely heavily on the labeling system outlined in #1 above. Using the `label:` designation, you can perform Boolean searches on the contents of your Gmail account. Here are some examples:

- To search for more than one label (siegfried and roy):
  `label:siegfried AND label:roy`
- To search for one label or another:
  `label:siegfried OR label:roy`
- To search for one label but not another:
  `label:siegfried AND NOT label:roy`

4. Searching query words

If you click the Show Search Options link of the main Gmail page, you get to a Search Options dialog box.

In the Search Options dialog box, you can specify the usual search parameters like From or To a certain address or e-mail with a particular subject line, and even designate whether the e-mail is read or unread. If you are looking for that one incriminating photo attachment of your spouse, you can set parameters like "must have an attachment and have been received within these dates."

While this GUI interface has many options, there are even more available to those who want to master the query operators that govern the Google search box. For example, you could type this search:

```
label:siegfried AND NOT label:roy has:attachment before:2005/11/17
```

That search would find e-mails labeled Siegfried and not Roy, with attachments, and dated before November 17, 2005.

Table A shows you a complete list of query operators that you can use in advanced searching.

5. Import contacts

After getting a Gmail account, one of the first things you are probably going to do is port over your contacts from your other e-mail clients like Outlook or Eudora. The Gmail contacts upload wizard will accept contact lists in comma-separated values (CSV) format, which means just about any other client, if it can generate a CSV list, is fair game for importing into Gmail. The only caveat to remember is that Gmail contacts use a limited number of fields: name, e-mail address, and notes. All the fields beyond name and e-mail address will be transferred into the notes field.

6. Rich formatting

E-mail composed in the Gmail service is defaulted to be saved and sent in the Rich Text Format (RTF). This means that most of the e-mail clients receiving your sent e-mail will be able to see formatting without having to render and display HTML. Many security conscious recipients refuse HTML encoded e-mail out of hand, without even looking at it because of the inherent security risks associated with worms and viruses.

Table A

Operator	Definition	Example(s)
from:	Used to specify the sender	Example - **from:amy** Meaning - Messages from Amy
to:	Used to specify a recipient	Example - **to:david** Meaning - All messages that were sent to David (by you or someone else)
subject:	Search for words in the subject line	Example - **subject:dinner** Meaning - Messages that have the word "dinner" in the subject
OR	Search for messages matching term A or term B *OR must be in all caps	Example - **from:amy OR from:david** Meaning - Messages from Amy or from David
- (hyphen)	Used to exclude messages from your search	Example - **dinner -movie** Meaning - Messages that contain the word "dinner" but do not contain the word "movie"
label:	Search for messages by label *There isn't a search operator for unlabeled messages	Example - **from:amy label:friends** Meaning - Messages from Amy that have the label "friends" Example - **from:david label:my-family** Meaning - Messages from David that have the label "My Family"
has:attachment	Search for messages with an attachment	Example - **from:david has:attachment** Meaning - Messages from David that have an attachment
filename:	Search for an attachment by name or type	Example - **filename:physicshomework.txt** Meaning - Messages with an attachment named "physicshomework.txt" Example - **label:work filename:pdf** Meaning - Messages labeled "work" that also have a PDF file as an attachment

“ ” (quotes)	Used to search for an exact phrase *Capitalization isn’t taken into consideration	Example - **“i’m feeling lucky”** Meaning - Messages containing the phrase “i’m feeling lucky” or “I’m feeling lucky” Example - **subject:“dinner and a movie”** Meaning - Messages containing the phrase “dinner and a movie” in the subject
( )	Used to group words Used to specify terms that shouldn’t be excluded	Example - **from:amy(dinner OR movie)** Meaning - Messages from Amy that contain either the word “dinner” or the word “movie” Example - **subject:(dinner movie)** Meaning - Messages in which the subject contains both the word “dinner” and the word “movie”
in:anywhere	Search for messages anywhere in your account *Messages in ‘Spam’ and ‘Trash’ are excluded from searches by default	Example - **in:anywhere subject:movie** Meaning - Messages in ‘All Mail,’ ‘Spam,’ and ‘Trash’ that contain the word “movie”
in:inbox **in:trash** **in:spam**	Search for messages in ‘Inbox,’ ‘Trash,’ or ‘Spam’	Example - **in:trash from:amy** Meaning - Messages from Amy that are in the trash
is:starred **is:unread** **is:read**	Search for messages that are starred, unread, or read	Example - **is:read is:starred from:David** Meaning - Messages from David that have been read and are marked with a star
cc: **bcc:**	Used to specify recipients in the ‘cc’ or ‘bcc’ fields *Search on bcc: cannot retrieve messages on which you were blind carbon copied<>	Example - **cc:david** Meaning - Messages that were cc-ed to David
after: **before:**	Search for messages sent during a certain period of time *Dates must be in yyyy/mm/dd format.	Example - **after:2004/04/16 before:2004/04/18** Meaning - Messages sent after April 16, 2004, but before April 18, 2004. *More precisely: Messages sent on April 17, 2004.

To help you create your fancy formatted e-mail documents, Gmail includes several common word processing features on the composition toolbar including bold, italic, text color, bullet points, and hyper linking. If you prefer, you can remove the formatting and send your message in plain text.

7. Built-in security

Gmail offers an SSL-encrypted login by default, which means entering your password for access to Gmail is a protected transfer of information. Encrypted login is probably something you would expect, but you can add another layer of protection by adding an "S" to your URL request. Using this link to get to your Gmail account will activate secure HTTPS access: https://gmail.google.com/.

8. View attachments

When you receive an attached image in your Gmail account, you are presented with a thumbnail copy of the image and given two choices for viewing it. You can choose to view the image, and Gmail will show it to you there in your browser, or you can choose to download it to your personal PC for viewing later in an application designed for image and photo manipulation.

9. Spelling

For those of us who are correct spelling challenged the invention of the spell-checker inside word processors ranks as one of the greatest feature enhancements of all time. The lack of a spell checker in most Web-based e-mail services is probably the one feature that made the prospect of using those services daunting and kept us away in droves. Google has addressed that concern by adding a very good spell checker to the e-mail composition interface. Click the spell check button and the system will scan your e-mail, mark what it perceives to be misspellings, and then suggest possible changes.

10. Forwarding and POP access

In this always on, always connected, technology-driven world in which we live, being away from your e-mail is just not acceptable anymore. To help you keep in touch with your Gmail account you can forward whatever e-mail you receive to another e-mail client and you can use the POP3 protocol to retrieve the e-mail sitting in your inbox from another client. Both of these functions can be accessed from the Mail Settings dialog box.

More tips

This is just a short list of Gmail's many features. The power and sophisticated feature set of the Gmail service is remarkable, especially when you consider this is all processed from your browser. Now you can truly get e-mail from just about anywhere—all you need is a PC and an Internet connection. Is it any wonder that the Internet Café has become so popular around the world? ❖

10 things you should know about the NETSH tool

By Rick Vanover

NETSH is one of the most powerful tools in the Windows networking toolkit. This list will introduce you to some good uses of NETSH in various scenarios and show you how you can streamline your networking configuration, administration, and documentation.

1. What is NETSH?

NETSH is one of the most powerful yet least known networking tools included with Windows 2000 and Windows Server 2003. It's installed by default and is located in the %systemroot%\system32 folder. NETSH is also available on Windows XP.

NETSH enables you to display, modify, import, and export many aspects of the network parameters of a system. It can also connect remotely to other systems with a remote machine parameter (-r).

2. Contexts for NETSH

Contexts are specific dimensions of the network configuration that can be managed by NETSH. The commands and options within NETSH are context sensitive, and the same command may exist in multiple context areas but have different commands and results in each context. Here are the Windows Server 2003 NETSH context areas:

Context	Description
aaaa	Authentication, authorization, accounting, and auditing
dhcp	DHCP server administration
diag	OS and network service parameters
interface	NIC configuration; includes subcontexts
ipsec	Alternative to IP Security Policy Management
netsh bridge	Network bridging configuration
ras	Remote access server configuration
routing	Routing administration (instead of RRAS)
rpc	Subnet and interface settings
wins	Windows Internet Name Service administration

Now, to add to the confusion, a context can have a subcontext. For example, the `interface` context has three subcontexts: `ip`, `ipv6`, and `portproxy`. NETSH refers to these subcontexts as a context, such as the `netsh interface ip` context. Note that Windows XP has a different set of contexts. When using the import and export operations in noninteractive mode, you must specify context or subcontext configuration.

3. Coordinating network change control with NETSH

You can use NETSH to export and import network configurations. A good example of using NETSH with networking change control would be when a system is going to be placed on a different network, but the communication channels need to be maintained to various other systems. A NETSH export will allow all parties to agree on various network settings. For example, consider the following portion of a NETSH export of the interface context from a dump operation:

```
set address name = "Teamed NIC" source = static addr =
   10.64.32.100 mask = 255.255.252.0

set address name = "Teamed NIC" gateway = 10.25.44.1 gwmetric = 1

set dns name = "Teamed NIC" source = static addr = 10.64.22.50

add dns name = "Teamed NIC" addr = 10.95.61.22

add dns name = "Teamed NIC" addr = 10.95.45.34

set wins name = "Teamed NIC" source = static addr = 10.95.45.70

add wins name = "Teamed NIC" addr = 10.95.45.25
```

Reviewing a NETSH export with all parties involved can ensure that the system will be routed correctly, using the correct DNS, WINS, and subnet mask. The best part is that you can then import the entire file into the Windows system after all appropriate entries have been made without any chance of entering the information incorrectly. And this is only for the interface context. The same applies for all other context scripts.

4. Using NETSH to dynamically change TCP/IP addresses

You can use NETSH to make dynamic IP address changes from a static IP address to DHCP simply by importing a file. NETSH can also bring in the entire Layer-3 configuration (TCP/IP Address, DNS settings, WINS settings, IP aliases, etc.). This can be handy when you're working on networks without DHCP and have a mobile computer that connects to multiple networks, some of which have DHCP. NETSH shortcuts will far exceed the capabilities of using Windows Automatic Pubic IP Addressing. Here is an example of running a dynamic update of an IP address:

```
C:\NETSH -f filename.netsh
```

In this example, filename.netsh is the NETSH file that contains an interface dump configuration. You can make shortcuts in Windows to a .BAT file that will run that command so you can easily add shortcuts to get a DHCP address and switch to a static IP address for a customer site, DMZ network, or any other static IP network.

5. Best practice: Using a .NETSH extension

NETSH import and export operations are in a native plain text format and can be read and edited from any text tool. However, NETSH files should be handled as a special file type because they're used to document network configurations, as well as for the import and export process. A best practice would be to make all export operations refer to a FILE.NETSH, where this file is what has been exported from NETSH. This is especially important because a NETSH export file doesn't contain the word NETSH in it. This way, even a novice can figure out what the file contains.

The file extension from export (dump) and import (-f) operations are entirely user specified. For convenience, you can associate the .NETSH extension with your Windows installation to allow native double-click editing.

6. NETSH in interactive mode

NETSH is one of the Windows tools that can be run in either an interactive or a noninteractive environment. Interactive tools (such as nslookup and dnscmd) have effectively different usage scenarios depending on the mode chosen.

Interactive mode also has two submodes: online and offline. Online mode is a direct interaction with the networking components while in interactive mode. Offline mode lets you interactively make changes and then roll them all online instantly by going to online mode.

7. NETSH in noninteractive mode

In noninteractive mode, you can implement NETSH commands by importing a file. Using noninteractive mode is recommended for file import and export operations. With NETSH in noninteractive mode, you can export key settings from each context as a specific aspect of your system documentation. In addition, if an issue arises and you can trace it back to a specific networking topic for which you have a NETSH script exported from a known working time, you can re-import that NETSH script in noninteractive mode and restore your networking functionality to that point. Please note that NETSH does not back up data within the contexts, such as the WINS database.

8. Clarifying the scripts

When exchanging NETSH scripts, you can insert comments to solicit feedback. This will allow you to explain an entry or use it as a training tool for others. Simply insert REM in a NETSH exported file to add a comment. Don't put in too many comments, however; just what is necessary.

9. NETSH precautions

NETSH is a powerful tool and should be used with caution. Using interactive online mode (the default) for changes on the fly can be more risky than implementing a change in interactive offline mode and going online to commit the changes. However, using noninteractive mode to perform changes is popular as well because the changes can be scripted. Try your hand at NETSH on a virtual machine or test system first.

10. Navigating NETSH

The large array of features available in NETSH may seem overwhelming at first. It's helpful to get into NETSH to see the options available and practice using the interface in interactive mode (a little different for those of us used to noninteractive tools). Getting into NETSH in interactive mode is easy: Simply type *NETSH* at the command prompt. Then, use these guidelines to investigate the command options:

- To change to another context, type the name of the context. For example, typing `interface ip` will go immediately to the `interface ip` context from whichever context you are presently located.
- To change your mode, type *offline* or *online*. Typing *offline* will send the interactive session offline, so any changes won't be brought in immediately. Typing *online* will bring the interactive session online, so changes will immediately be brought into the networking elements of the system.
- Typing *show mode* will display the current mode (offline or online). The default mode is online, so be sure to immediately jump offline if you are experimenting.
- Typing *?* or *help* will show the available commands for your current context location. If you're in the root of the tool, there is no active context and your interface to the tool will be a `netsh>` prompt.
- Global commands, such as `online` and `quit`, are those you can use everywhere. Context commands are available only in the current context. For example, from the `netsh interface ip>` context, you can view the network configuration by running show dns, but this command may not work other contexts or sub-contexts.
- In contexts, running `set` and `show` will provide the context-sensitive command options. ❖

10 things you should know about working with Microsoft Access reports

By Susan Harkins

When you need to share database information in a consistent and easy-to-read manner, you can use Access' reporting features to present the relevant data in printed format. Setting up a report is a fairly straightforward process, but knowing some of these tips and tricks will help you work more efficiently and generate better results.

1. Build a group header.

If you group data numerically or alphabetically, you may want a visual clue that the group is changing. For instance, you might want to print A, B, C, and so on, at the beginning of alphabetically grouped sections. In the Group section, use a calculated control with the following expression as the control's Control Source property: `=Left(nameoffield, 1)`, where *nameoffield* is the field by which the section is grouped.

2. Create a no-hassle title page.

If your report needs a title page, you don't have to create it separately—use the Report Header instead. Add the text and graphics you want to appear in the title page to the Report Header section. Then, set the Report Header's Force New Property to the After Section setting. That way, Access will force the data following the Report Header to a new page. The report prints this section just once, so it's a great spot for title page information. You'll probably need to tweak the text and graphics in the Report Header section until you get things arranged the way you want them, but that's a one-time job.

3. Enhance reports with chart summaries.

Given the graphic nature of reports, charts are a great way to summarize the reported data. The good news is that you can use the Chart Wizard to add a chart to a report. With the report in Design View, choose Chart from the Insert menu and position the chart in the report. This will launch the Chart Wizard. Position the chart in the Report Header or Footer or a Group Header or Footer to graphically summarize the data.

4. Omit unwanted extra pages.

Sometimes, a report prints a blank page between each page or every other page. Usually, this blank page indicates that the report is wider than the paper you've selected. It's easy to extend a control or line past the margin and not even know it—and it's hard to find the offending object. An easy way to spot the problem is to click the horizontal ruler at the right margin to select all of the controls that appear close to the margin. If you're lucky, it'll be just a few, and the one that's extending just a bit beyond that margin will be much easier to spot with the selection handles showing. Once you find the object, simply adjust its size.

5. Print custom messages.

Conditional formatting lets you base formats on the value itself. For instance, a negative value appears in red; a positive value appears in black. Rather than formatting, you may want to print a particular message to yourself or the reader. For instance, if a certain customer hasn't ordered for a while, you may want a visual clue that reads "Call Customer for Chat." You can accomplish this by adding a text box (most likely in the Detail section) and using an `Iif()` function in the form

```
Iif(conditionismet, "printthismessage")
```

6. Save time with automatic formats.

You can spend a lot of time formatting a report. Fortunately, if your specifications are consistent throughout the same database, you don't need to reformat each one. Save your finished report as an AutoFormat and then apply that AutoFormat to new reports.

First, with the finished report in Design View, choose AutoFormat from the Format menu. Then, click the Customize button, check the Create A New AutoFormat Based On The Report 'Reportname' option, and click OK. Now, enter a name for the new AutoFormat and click OK. To apply the AutoFormat to a new report, choose AutoFormat from the Format menu, select the custom item from the Reports AutoFormats list, and click OK.

7. Add line numbers.

You can easily add a line number to detail records in a report. In Design View, add an unbound text box to the Detail section—usually to the left of the controls. Enter the expression =1 as the new control's Control Source property. Then, change the control's Running Sum property to Over All for reports that aren't grouped. If you want numbering to be exclusive to a group, use the Over Group setting.

8. Use identifying expressions.

Reports aren't limited to the data in the data source. You might want to print the report's name or the location of the database somewhere on your report. To do so, just add a calculated control, typically to the report's Header or Footer section, and use one of the following expressions:

`=CurrentObjectName` prints the report's name

`=CurrentDB.Name & " " & CurrentObjectName` prints the report's complete pathname

9. Place a border around your report.

You can display borders around controls and report sections, but there's no built-in feature that prints a border around the perimeter of your report. To do that you'll need to add the following code to the report's Page event:

```
Private Sub Report_Page()

  Me.Line(0,0)-Me(Me.ScaleWidth, Me.ScaleHeight), , B

End Sub
```

10. Cancel an empty report.

Just because you have a report, that doesn't mean it will include data. Sometimes, the criteria filter out all the records and you end up with an empty report. Instead of viewing an empty report, you can cancel it by adding the following VBA code to the report's No Data event:

```
Private Sub Report_NoData(Cancel As Integer)

  MsgBox "There are no records to display"

  Cancel = True

End Sub
```

❖

10 things you should know about PowerPoint abuse

by Jesper Johansson

These suggestions are taken from the blog posting "Death by PowerPoint" written by Jesper Johansson (http://techrepublic.com.com/5254-6257-0.html?forumID=99&threadID=181286&messageID=1847623&id=4224622).

I'm at yet another event, and this time I decided to go see a few of the other sessions instead of just trying to find as much free food as possible between my own presentations. This experience brought to mind an old concept: "Death by PowerPoint." It is almost embarrassing how some people use PowerPoint. Steve Riley (http://blogs.technet.com/steriley) frequently refers to e-mail as "the place where knowledge goes to die." Well Steve, you have it wrong. Nothing kills knowledge as fast as putting it in PowerPoint. Here are some of the most egregious ways of using PowerPoint that I've seen.

1. PowerPoint is NOT a word processor!

The point of a PowerPoint slide is not to cram as much information into a single slide as possible. The idea of a slide is to have memory joggers that trigger thinking in the audience. That means you do not need to even have complete sentences (although it is a bonus if the words are spelled correctly). Simple statements work just fine.

2. Most of your audience probably knows how to read.

A corollary to the thinking that PowerPoint is a word processor is that far too many presenters stand on stage reading the slides. It turns out that most of the audience members probably are literate and can read the slides for themselves. The purpose of a presentation is not to do so for them. If you want to read to people, go to the reading hour at the local library. A presentation is about explaining things to people that go above and beyond what they get in the slides. If it weren't, they might just as well get your slides and read them in the comfort of their own office, home, boat, or bathroom.

3. A picture is worth a thousand words, possibly more.

Just because PowerPoint has bullets is no reason to use them. There is no way you can convey as much information in a slide full of bullets as you can in a slide with a single picture on it. Try this next time: Put a picture in instead of the bullets and then talk about the picture. People will find it much more interesting and much more informative. As a bonus, it makes it more worthwhile to come to the presentation as opposed to just downloading the slides, making you a more important person to have at the event.

4. It's a good idea to know your presentation.

Statements like "Oops, what is that slide doing here" or "I don't really know what this point is trying to say" are never a good thing in a presentation. Generally speaking, an audience that went through the time and effort to attend your presentation expects you to have spent at least that much time preparing for it. Taking someone else's presentation and just standing up and reading the slides as they show up is typically not going to work out too well.

5. Bullets are bad, stories are good.

There is no law that says everything you say has to fit in a bullet. In fact, teaching by bullet points was never one of the more interesting approaches in school, was it? Think back to the classes that you enjoyed. Most of the time they were the ones where the teacher related the material to real life by telling a story that illustrated the points. Which would you rather hear? A sound-bite explanation of the four pieces that need to be proven in a lawsuit over negligence or a story about how someone was negligent and got sued over it?

6. The actual content of your presentation is much more important than the slide show template you used!

I do about 80 conference presentations a year. For some reason, every single event feels that it must have a unique PowerPoint template for its slides. It takes anywhere from 15 minutes to two hours to reapply a template, depending on the presentation and what you have done in it. That is two hours that could be profitably spent doing other things—like, say, putting in content that the audience cares about as opposed to setting it in a template they don't care about. That is two weeks of my time a year when I can't create information and transfer knowledge but instead have to spend trying to figure out why somebody decided that a red font on a blue background was a good idea.

7. The purpose of the three-pane view is not so you can see which the next slide is.

PowerPoint's three-pane view is great—for building presentations. It is not there as a substitute for rehearsals so you can tell which the next slide is. Hit [F5] and use PowerPoint the way it was designed. If you're already in three-pane view by the time you read this, hit [Shift][F5] and that will start the slideshow from the current slide.

8. Don't put your audience in pain.

Okay, so the general idea is to transfer knowledge. If you make the audience's collective eyes bleed by putting up white slides with a black font, something that is just horribly painful to look at in a dark room, you are much less likely to actually convey any points since they will be trying to look away from the screen the whole time. Also… **It is not a requirement to have at least one slide in each presentation that nobody can read.** Contrary to public opinion, you don't have to have a slide that nobody can read. That's what handouts are for. If people can't read it, why put it on the screen? Why waste the audience's time with it?

9. Be conscious of people with disabilities.

Most disabilities do not interfere with a presentation. However, some do. For instance, red text on a blue background is impossible to see for people who are colorblind since it won't stop moving. Red text on black has the same effect, and red text on green simply disappears unless they are completely red-green, in which case the red text just jumps around a lot instead.

10. Twelve-point font is not appropriate.

Twelve-point font can't be read unless you are right in front of the slide, in which case you need to move your head far too much. Fourteen points is bare minimum. Ideally, don't go below 18. Also… there's no contest to see who can use the most fonts. You won't get dinged if you don't use 12 fonts in a single slide. One or two is perfectly fine and actually makes the slide readable instead—an extra bonus. ❖

15 things DBAs should unlearn about Oracle

By Bob Watkins

Database administrators, like most professionals, tend to keep doing those things that have worked in the past. Over time, these practices take on a life of their own, passing down from DBA to DBA like folklore. But all products move on, adding new features, and the Oracle database is no exception. Major new features were introduced in versions 8*i*, 9*i*, and 10*g* that call for a reexamination of what "everybody knows" about Oracle. Let's take a look at 15 cherished beliefs Oracle DBAs hold and why these beliefs may no longer be true.

1. Block size is fixed.

The fundamental unit of storage in Oracle is the block—the smallest amount of data Oracle can read or write at a time. A block size—2, 4, 8, 16, or 32 KB—is chosen when the database is initially created and is used both for the physical disk space and buffers in memory. Most DBAs believe that once the block size is chosen, it can't be altered without reloading the database, and that it applies to all tablespaces in the database. Neither is true starting with Oracle 9i.

Each tablespace may now use a different block size. It's done like this:

```
CREATE TABLESPACE book_data

BLOCKSIZE 8K

DATAFILE '/u3/oradata/prod/bookdata01.dbf' SIZE 100M;
```

You can check which block sizes are in use via the new BLOCK_SIZE column in the DBA_TABLESPACES and V$DATAFILE views.

If you use a different block size from the default for the database, you must set up a memory cache for it using the initialization parameter file. Six new parameters are defined. db_cache_size replaces db_block_buffers to indicate the size of the buffer cache for default-sized blocks. db_2k_cache_size indicates the buffer cache size for 2-KB blocks, if such blocks are nonstandard for the database. There are 4-KB, 8-KB, 16-KB, and 32-KB versions as well. Unlike their predecessor, db_block_buffers, these parameters are all measured in bytes, not the number of buffers to allocate.

2. Single extent tables are faster.

Oracle DBA folklore says that the best input/output (I/O) performance is achieved when all the blocks for a table are in a single contiguous extent. This one is true—sometimes. But not for the reason you might expect.

In a white paper titled "How to Stop Defragmenting and Start Living" (http://otn.oracle.com/deploy/availability/pdf/defrag.pdf—free registration required), Bhaskar Himatsingka and Juan Loaiza of Oracle Corporation argue that multiextent tables don't necessarily perform worse than single-extent ones. What matters, they assert, is the size of the extents. Given a large enough extent size, the Oracle engine can preread efficiently even across multiple extents.

To best use this insight, the authors recommend that the DBA standardize on three extent sizes and use them exclusively in all tables: 128 KB for small tables, 4 MB for medium tables, and 128 MB for only the largest tables. Using 128-KB extent sizes may seem to waste space, but the cost of this wasted space is trivial compared to the cost of DBA time fussing over each individual storage allocation. These principles have been built in to the new Oracle 8i feature, Locally Managed Tablespaces.

3. Export and Import are the only ways to reorganize tables.

Seasoned DBAs will tell you that when a table needs to be moved, reorganized, or defragmented, it's a painful process. First, the table must be exported to an external "dump" file. The original table must then be dropped, optionally re-created manually in some cases, and finally imported again from the dump file. All this work may be unnecessary as of Oracle 8i.

Using the new MOVE clause in the ALTER TABLE enables you to change the tablespace and/or storage parameters of an Oracle table without using EXPORT and IMPORT. It looks like this:

```
ALTER TABLE author MOVE

TABLESPACE book_data

STORAGE (INITIAL 128K NEXT 128K PCTINCREASE 0);
```

In this case, the TABLESPACE clause tells Oracle to move the author table from its current tablespace to the book_data tablespace. The STORAGE clause works the same as for CREATE TABLE, indicating how large an extent to allocate and its growth properties. Either TABLESPACE or STORAGE is optional, enabling you to move the table without reorganizing it, and vice versa. Caution: In version 8i, the table will be locked for the entire duration of the ALTER TABLE command, so it's still best to do such work during nonpeak hours. In version 9i, that restriction is lifted. When you add the word ONLINE to the syntax, the table can be moved even while users are updating it.

Also, note that you must have enough disk space for two copies of the table: the old one and the new. Oracle doesn't drop the old table until the new one is completely built. If your table is too big for this approach, you'll have to do it the old-fashioned way with Export and Import.

4. Columns can't be dropped.

Oracle DBAs have gotten used to the fact that once a column has been defined for a table, it can't be renamed or dropped. To get rid of it, you have to create a new table without the column and then load that table with data from the original. Finally, you have to reset all permissions, indexes, triggers, etc., on the new table that were on the original one. Not anymore. Starting in Oracle 9i R1, you can drop a column and add the correct one instead. The SET UNUSED and DROP clauses of the ALTER TABLE command are used for this. Here's an example:

```
ALTER TABLE author
DROP (birthplace, birthyear);

ALTER TABLE author
SET UNUSED (birthhospital);
```

Both clauses permanently delete a column. The only difference occurs when Oracle does its cleanup. A column that is set to unused disappears from the data dictionary, so users can't reference it. But the physical space is still taken up until manually cleared by the DBA. With the DROP option, the reorganization is done immediately. The SET UNUSED option allows the DBA to make the column unavailable immediately, without inconveniencing users with the overhead of cleanup.

Caution: All data contained in the column is irretrievably lost when a column is marked unused or dropped. These are data definition language (DDL) commands, so there is no ROLLBACK. Be careful and have good backups!

5. Stored procedures always run as the owner.

When an Oracle user is given the permission to execute a stored procedure, he or she is implicitly given permission to do whatever that stored procedure does. No matter how many tables the procedure updates or how it updates them (even deleting rows), the user can do it. In other words, the user obtains all the rights of the owner while running the procedure. Starting with Oracle 8i, however, a stored procedure can be created with either the rights of the owner or the rights of the person executing it. You use the AUTHID clause of the CREATE PROCEDURE command for this. For example:

```
CREATE PROCEDURE count_authors
  (num_books OUT NUMBER)
  AUTHID CURRENT_USER
IS
  SELECT COUNT(*) INTO num_books
  FROM author;
END;
```

A stored procedure defined as AUTHID CURRENT_USER will allow access to a table only if the user owns the table or has been given permission to use it. Furthermore, references to unqualified table names, like author in the example above, refer to the user's copy of author, not the original owner's. The currently logged-in user's schema, or list of objects, is used to resolve references.

6. Only the DBA can recover data.

People who work directly in the SQL language—DBAs and IT consultants—can corrupt or lose data with one mistyped command. In fact, user error is the most common reason for database downtime, according to Oracle. A table dropped from the production database instead of development can bring an application and all its users to an abrupt halt. Even an improper update can corrupt the results reported from a database. Recovering from such errors used to be a time-consuming job that only the DBA could perform. But since Oracle 9i, users can fix many such errors themselves via SQL commands. The mechanism for this is the new 9i feature called Flashback Query. Here's an example using the sample data in the SCOTT schema (http://otn.oracle.com/oramag/oracle/02-jul/o42schema.html). An employee record is deleted, and the change committed:

```
DELETE FROM emp WHERE empno = 7934;
COMMIT;
```

The row is missing from further SELECT statements, and even a ROLLBACK command cannot bring the row back. However, a Flashback Query can display the contents of the table as it was 10 minutes ago, when the deleted row still existed:

```
SELECT * FROM emp
  AS OF TIMESTAMP (SYSTIMESTAMP - INTERVAL '10' MINUTE)
WHERE empno = 7934;
```

This SELECT statement can be used as the subquery of an INSERT statement to reload the deleted data. Be aware, however, that INSERT will be subject to any constraints on the table and that any INSERT triggers on the table will be executed. To set the entire session to flash back to a particular point in time, use the DBMS_FLASHBACK package:

```
EXEC DBMS_FLASHBACK.ENABLE_AT_TIME(TIMESTAMP
  'yyyy-mm-ddhh:mi:ss');
```

Data accessed during a flashback session cannot be modified, only read. It's just like science fiction stories involving time travel: You can visit the past, but you can't change it! To return the session to the present, type:

```
EXEC DBMS_FLASHBACK.DISABLE;
```

For Flashback Query to work, the database must be using Automated Undo Management (AUM), and an undo tablespace must be created. The amount of time a user can flash back is limited by the initialization parameter undo_retention and the size of the undo tablespace. Although this feature is a godsend for IT consultants, Oracle's intent is for any user who directly types SQL to be able to recover from his or her own errors. Flashback is an object privilege, so it can be granted on individual tables or to all tables via the system privilege

```
FLASHBACK ANY TABLE
```

But wait: it gets better! In version 9i, Flashback is limited to Data Manipulation Language (DML) commands such as SELECT, INSERT, UPDATE, and DELETE. But in Oracle 10g, even a dropped table can be recovered via Flashback.

7. Oracle can't store fractions of seconds.

Oracle's DATE datatype has always stored time to the nearest full second. Developers needing more precise time measurements use the NUMBER datatype instead. This practice makes computing time intervals difficult.

Starting with version 9i, Oracle includes an enhanced date/time datatype consistent with the 1999 SQL standard. To declare such a column, use the TIMESTAMP datatype and indicate the number of fractional digits desired (the default is 6):

```
CREATE TABLE event_ts (
  event_id  NUMBER(6)
  ,event_name VARCHAR2(40)
  ,start_time TIMESTAMP(2)
  ,elapsed_time TIMESTAMP(2)
);
```

A TIMESTAMP literal, like a DATE literal, must be enclosed in single quotes. Unlike dates, however, the word TIMESTAMP is required as well. The following literal represents March 23, 2004, at a half-second past midnight:

```
TIMESTAMP '2004-03-23 00:00:00.50'
```

Although the standard DATE literal doesn't include time, the standard format for a TIMESTAMP literal requires it. The session parameter NLS_TIMESTAMP_FORMAT controls the format, in the same way that NLS_DATE_FORMAT sets the standard DATE format. A new conversion function, TO_TIMESTAMP, creates a TIMESTAMP from other input formats, and the TO_CHAR function has been enhanced to display a TIMESTAMP's components in any order.

To obtain the current date and time in TIMESTAMP format, use the SYSTIMESTAMP function instead of SYSDATE. For example:

```
SELECT SYSTIMESTAMP FROM DUAL;
```

8. A corrupted block requires dropping an object.

IT consultants dread the Oracle error message ORA-1578, *Oracle data block corrupted.* The internal structure of one of the database's blocks is no longer correct. The message identifies the block in error by file number and block number. The cure has always been to run a query such as:

```
SELECT owner, segment_name, segment_type
FROM dba_extents
WHERE file_id = <filenumber>
AND <blocknumber> BETWEEN block_id AND block_id + blocks - 1;
```

where *<filenumber>* and *<blocknumber>* were the numbers from the error message. This query indicates which object contains the corrupted block. Then, depending on the object type, recovery is either straightforward (for indexes and temporary segments), messy (for tables), or very messy (for active rollback segments and parts of the data dictionary).

In Oracle 9i Enterprise Edition, however, a new Recovery Manager (RMAN) command, BLOCKRECOVER, can repair the block in place without dropping and re-creating the object involved. After logging in to RMAN and connecting to the target database, type:

```
BLOCKRECOVER DATAFILE <filenumber> BLOCK <blocknumber>;
```

A new view, V$DATABASE_BLOCK_CORRUPTION, gets updated during RMAN backups, and a block must be listed as corrupt for a BLOCKRECOVER to be performed. To recover all blocks that have been marked corrupt, the following RMAN sequence can be used:

```
BACKUP VALIDATE DATABASE;
BLOCKRECOVER CORRUPTION LIST;
```

This approach is efficient if only a few blocks need recovery. For large-scale corruption, it's more efficient to restore a prior image of the datafile and recover the entire datafile, as before. As with any new feature, test it carefully before using it on a production database.

9. Columns can't be renamed or reorganized.

Renaming a table column or changing its data type usually meant creating a new table and copying the old data to it. Columns couldn't be renamed at all, and datatypes could be changed only if they had no data (only NULL values).

Oracle 9i has not one but two ways to overcome these limitations. The ALTER TABLE command can now rename columns directly:

```
ALTER TABLE books RENAME COLUMN tiitle TO title;
```

Function-based indexes and constraints will automatically use the new column name. However, code objects such as views, triggers, procedures, and functions will be invalidated by the change and must be recompiled. Be sure to assess the impact of a renamed column on your code before doing it! Of course, if you have just created a table and there are no dependent objects, this is a quick fix for bad typing.

A supplied PL/SQL package called DBMS_REDEFINITION enables a DBA to change a table's column structure while the table is online and available to users. It's a complex procedure, but in general the steps are as follows:

1. Use DBMS_REDEFINITION.CAN_REDEF_TABLE to check whether the table qualifies for online redefinition, and specify whether the redefinition will be by primary key (recommended) or by row IDs.
2. Create an empty table in the same schema, but with the desired layout. Omit columns you want to drop; include new columns you'd like to create.
3. Use DBMS_REDEFINITION.START_REDEF_TABLE to begin the redefinition process. The parameters to this procedure indicate the old table, the new one, and the mapping of the existing columns to the columns of the new table.
4. Create any constraints (disabled), triggers, indexes, and grants desired on the new table.
5. Use DBMS_REDEFINITION.FINISH_REDEF_TABLE to complete the process. The original table is locked for a short time regardless of how large or small it is, while the definitions are swapped between the two tables.
6. Drop the temporary table used in the redefinition; it is no longer needed.

Of course, redefining a table doesn't automatically update any application code that accesses that table. Applications must be changed and tested separately. What DBMS_REDEFINITION does, however, is shorten the time that the table is unavailable to users at cutover time.

10. Only the owner of a table can grant permission to use it.

When I explained Oracle security in prior versions, clients couldn't believe that the DBA could not grant permissions on a table unless the table's owner had first granted it to the DBA. Historically, however, this has been the case. The restriction was part of Oracle's design, but it made administration difficult. In Oracle 9i, a new system privilege changes this.

The DBA role now has a system privilege called GRANT ANY OBJECT PRIVILEGE. In the past, a statement like

```
GRANT SELECT ON scott.emp TO giselle;
```

would fail unless SCOTT had first granted the DBA the SELECT privilege on his table WITH GRANT OPTION. Now, that same statement will work. This privilege can also be used by lead developers to grant permission on a schema's objects without having to log in as that schema's owner.

11. The only wildcards in SQL are % and _.

When doing pattern match queries with the LIKE operator, both DBAs and developers have learned to put up with having only two wildcard characters at their disposal: percent, which matches anything, and underscore, which matches any one character. For more elaborate matching, they would write PL/SQL.

Starting with Oracle 10g, this extra coding is no longer needed. A full set of regular expression syntax, such as used in UNIX shell scripting, is now available directly in SQL. Oracle supports the complete set of POSIX standard extended regular expressions (ERE). For a list of these expressions, see Appendix C of the Oracle 10g SQL Reference.

The operator REGEXP_LIKE replaces LIKE, and the regular expression must be quoted and in parentheses. For example, the following WHERE clause searches for A1, A2, or A3 occurring only at the beginning of a part number:

```
WHERE REGEXP_LIKE (partno, '^A[123]')
```

Notice that no * wildcard is needed at the end of the regular expression. Unlike the wildcards used with the LIKE operator, regular expressions assume a partial match unless you force a complete one. So the above expression will match "A1" and "A3," but also "A234." To force an exact match, use the $ to indicate end of line:

```
WHERE REGEXP_LIKE(partno, '^A[123]$')
```

The REGEXP_INSTR, REGEXP_SUBSTR, and REGEXP_REPLACE functions extend the INSTR, SUBSTR, and REPLACE functions to use regular expressions in the match argument. Again, the Oracle 10g SQL Reference describes these.

12. You have to rebuild a table to reset its High Water Mark.

End users often wonder why a table with few rows in it can take a long time to search. DBAs know that if the table used to have a lot of rows at one time, the search may be slow because Oracle has to look at every block that used to contain data—up to the table's High Water Mark, or HWM. They may also believe that the only way to reset the HWM is to rebuild the table, either via export/drop/import or ALTER TABLE MOVE.

In 10g, this is no longer necessary. A new feature called Online Segment Shrink can reclaim space in the table and adjust the HWM down as well. The syntax is:

```
ALTER TABLE tablename
  SHRINK SPACE [COMPACT] [CASCADE];
```

Giving this command without the options defragments the table, compacting the rows. It then adjusts the HWM to the new high position and releases the freed-up space.

The COMPACT option does the defragmentation but does not adjust the HWM nor release the storage space. The CASCADE option shrinks not only the named table, but any dependent objects, such as indexes.

And now, the fine print. The tablespace in which the table is stored must be set up for Automatic Segment Space Management, and the table itself must have row movement enabled. Because the moved rows will have new ROWIDs, you should turn off any triggers that fire based upon the ROWID, or they'll be re-executed. There are other restrictions as well: Consult the documentation.

13. Incomplete recoveries require restoring old data files.

Oracle DBAs know that Oracle recovers itself completely from instance failure upon startup and from physical failures, such as media failures, via the RECOVER command in RMAN or SQL*Plus. When a logical corruption occurs, however, they believe the only recourse is to restore the database files from backup taken before the problem occurred and to "roll forward" to the desired time via the redo logs.

In Oracle 10g, another option is possible: to roll back the database to a point in time prior to the damage, using the current data files. This feature can save a lot of time in an incomplete recovery scenario.

The Flashback feature introduced in Oracle 9i has been dramatically extended in 10g with FLASHBACK DATABASE (available as a command in RMAN and a statement in SQLPlus.) With the proper setup, you can now recover the database by rolling it backward from its current state, instead of rolling forward from an older image. This can be much faster, as it works with the existing data files. No old versions need to be restored. Flashing back the entire database is still an incomplete recovery: You will lose any data entered after the point in time to which you flash back. In brief, here's how to set it up:

1. Set aside a flash recovery area on disk large enough to hold the flashback database logs and other RMAN backups, such as control files. Set the parameters DB_RECOVERY_FILE_DEST and DB_RECOVERY_FILE_SIZE to tell the instance where to find it.
2. Set the DB_FLASHBACK_RETENTION_TARGET parameter to the number of minutes maximum that you want to be able to flash back.
3. Enable the flashback feature with the database in mount mode, with the command ALTER DATABASE FLASHBACK ON. Then ALTER the database open. The database will automatically begin backing up changed blocks on a regular basis to the flashback recovery area. Think of it as a continuous incremental backup at the block level.

If you need to flash back the database to an earlier time:

1. Place the instance in mount mode
2. Connect to the instance in RMAN and use the FLASHBACK DATABASE command. This command locates the most current block images before the flashback time you request and restores them. Then, it uses the redo logs to roll forward to the exact flashback time. Because the blocks are backed up fairly frequently, there is much less work to do to bring these blocks current. Plus, you avoid the entire time of restoring data files.

This technique is not appropriate for every instance, but like all insurance policies, you pay a little overhead on a regular basis to avoid a much bigger payout in case a problem occurs. For further information, consult the Oracle Database Backup and Recovery Advanced User's Guide, Chapter 9 ("Flashback Technology: Recovering from Logical Corruptions").

14. Tablespaces can be transported only to the same platform.

The transportable tablespace feature introduced in Oracle 8i enables datafiles to be copied directly from instance to instance. Because various operating systems store data in different byte orders ("endianness"), many DBAs believe you cannot transport tablespaces to an instance with a different block size or to a different hardware platform.

In Oracle 9i, the block size issue went away because you can have multiple block sizes in an instance. In Oracle 10g, the endianness problem also went away, because you can use RMAN to convert the endianness of the data. The result is a datafile copy targeted for a specific operating system. When such files are transported, they are already in the correct format necessary to plug in to another instance.

The RMAN command CONVERT is used for this. For example:

```
CONVERT TABLESPACE example TO PLATFORM 'HP-UX (64-bit)';
```

The view V$TRANSPORTABLE_PLATFORMS contains information about which are compatible and which require use of the CONVERT command.

The Database Administrator's Guide, Chapter 8 ("Managing Tablespaces") gives more details on transporting tablespaces.

15. CONNECT, RESOURCE, and DBA are a convenient way to set up users.

Many DBAs still use the CONNECT, RESOURCE, and DBA roles to set up new user accounts, either in automated scripts or manually, just by habit. Sometimes the things we have to unlearn are simple, comfortable things, like an old sweatshirt or pair of shoes that have long since worn out. These legacy roles were introduced in Oracle 7—yes, that's three major versions ago—as a bridge between the simple security model of Oracle 6 and the more granular one we have had since then. But that's all they were: a temporary convenience.

In computer security, the principle of least privilege says that users should have only the minimum privileges necessary to do their jobs. The CONNECT role, for example, includes system permissions such as CREATE TABLE and CREATE SEQUENCE, things that most end users are unlikely to need. The RESOURCE role contains the powerful UNLIMITED TABLESPACE privilege that overrides the tablespace quota system.

A better practice is to analyze the requirements of various job roles and create custom roles to match. Grant the required system and object privilege to these roles and then grant the roles to users. Grant users quotas on tablespaces only if they will be creating objects in those tablespaces. (Although quotas must be set directly on users and not roles, you can simplify the process in Enterprise Manager by using the "Create like" command to clone an existing user account.)

The bottom line

Our skills with Oracle are like the stocks in an investment portfolio. While most of us understand that we have to add new skills on a regular basis, it's not always obvious that there are some we should dump as well. Manage your portfolio well, and you'll have the most efficient set of tools to do the job. ❖

10 things you did not know about Lynx

By Mellonfire

Back before the <img> tag was invented, Web browsers were simple text readers, shorn of all the bells and whistles common today. And leading the pack was Lynx (http://lynx.isc.org/release/), a full-featured GPL text-mode browser that was as speedy as its namesake.

Today, Lynx is still a de facto part of many Linux installations and boasts a loyal fan following, especially among power users (who like the fact that it's fast and can be used without the overhead of a windowing system) and Web developers (who use it to check that their Web pages are readable in text mode). The biggest reason for its popularity is that under its unassuming exterior, Lynx comes with a very complete feature set, one that has helped it survive the onslaught of its prettier (and better-funded) competitors.

In this article, we'll be looking under the hood to introduce you to some of Lynx's less well-known capabilities. The tips discussed below apply to Lynx v2.8.5.

1. Turn on image links.

When viewing a page that you know contains images, turn on image links with the `<Shift>-8` key combination. Lynx will reload the page and include links for each image. You can then download and save the image(s) to disk using the links provided, or view them with an associated image viewer.

2. Navigate with a mouse.

Lynx supports mouse navigation if compiled with `ncurses` support. To activate this support, start Lynx with the `-use_mouse` option. You should now be able to click on links with the mouse cursor to activate them.

3. View HTML document source.

You can view the HTML source code of any page displayed in Lynx with the \ key, which toggles between source and rendered version. To save the source code of a page to disk, type *p* to choose from a list of save options.

4. Colorize page content.

You can color-code page content automatically in Lynx, by starting it with the `-color` option or by adding the directive `show_colors=always` to the Lynx configuration file. Once this setting is activated, directories, files, links, and images will be rendered in different colors for easy identification.

5. Edit local documents in one place.

Lynx can automatically invoke your favorite editor to edit local (not remote) documents. To activate this feature, first add the path to your text editor in the Lynx configuration file via the directive `file_editor`. Then, start Lynx with the name of the file you wish to edit, and type `e` to invoke edit mode.

6. Search for text in a page.

Type `/` to activate a search box and scan the page for matches to a search term. Matching terms will automatically be highlighted by Lynx. Use the `n` keystroke to proceed forward through the match list, and `N` to move backward.

7. Use bookmarks.

Like its graphical cousins, Lynx allows you to record your favorite sites to a bookmark list. Use the `a` keystroke to add a page to the bookmark list, and the `v` keystroke to view the current list.

8. Browse FTP sites.

Lynx comes with a fairly full-featured FTP client built in, making it a simple matter to browse FTP sites. To browse an FTP site, simply start Lynx with the complete FTP URL, in the format `ftp://user:pass@host:port/path/to/remote/dir/`. Lynx will attempt an FTP connection to the site and, if successful, will permit you to browse file listings and download individual files using the standard browser interface and key commands.

9. Crawl a Web site.

Start Lynx with the `-crawl` and `-traversal` command-line arguments, followed by the URL to traverse. Lynx will go to work traversing all links starting from the stated root node, saving the results to disk as independent pages. This is a great way to build a local mirror of an Internet site noninteractively.

10. Get help.

At any time, type *?* or *h* to obtain help. Lynx comes with a fair amount of online help, as well as links to other sites containing detailed FAQs and configuration information. ❖

10 quick tips on learning Microsoft Project

By Tom Bruner

Microsoft Project is a useful tool for any IT shop, regardless of size. And managers at any level, whether they're in the boardroom or the tech shop, can benefit from Project's efficient and effective features. For CIOs, it's a great tool for managing IT projects and achieving goals.

Here are 10 tips to help IT leaders who are new to using Microsoft Project.

1. Use it. No shop is too small for Project.

Even if you are a one-person shop, you can still use Project. If nothing else, it's a great tool to identify all of the tasks required to complete a project and the order in which they must be completed. If you only print out the task sheet, it makes a great checklist to keep you on track.

2. Follow the money.

The budget reports provided in Project will help you track spending on contractors. I usually don't assign costs to my staff because we're all salaried and as such a fixed cost. One neat trick is to set a resource for anything ordered—hardware, software, food, etc.—and then assign a cost to it. You can then use this to anticipate costs you will be incurring so your CFO can plan cash flow, budgets, etc.

Project includes a host of reports that apply to every aspect of the project. Frankly, I don't use them much in my work, but they do come in handy when the boss starts hitting you up for project information. Keep in mind that the most common question is "How much is all of this going to cost when all is said and done?"

3. Manage by monitoring project status and workloads.

You can insert Project files that pertain to several projects and manage your team schedule across several projects simultaneously. Scheduling conflicts between projects are more easily managed as well.

This feature came in handy recently when I had limited resources and three projects to complete at the same time. With Project you can create a master file for your total resource pool, then insert separate project files. I find this useful for dovetailing different projects—especially when a project is nearing completion. It also lets you manage preliminary planning for your next project. The application's functionality lets projects (and assignments) overlap for the same people on two projects and thus helps you avoid scheduling conflicts.

4. Estimate time needed and actual time used.

The application's Gantt chart has a bar for each task representing the time at which the task will be done and how long it will take. If you grab the left edge of a bar and drag, you can indicate how far along you are. If you run into problems (gee, that never happens) and the task is going to take longer, you can grab the right edge and extend the time needed.

5. Think big, then small.

Start with the one task, Upgrade Accounting System in this case, and then begin adding items.

After inserting more tasks and building detail, you can begin to assign tasks and set the amount of time you think it will take. Then assign who will be doing the work.

This is where the resource sheet comes in handy. Enter the names of the people with whom you'll be working. For consultants, you can also enter the billable rate for tracking.

Project's many features may overwhelm some new users. To be honest I can't even use them all. The beauty is that you are not constrained in Project—you don't have to use each feature to find benefit in the software. On small projects, I may typically use and refer to only a project Gantt chart.

Once you have a few basic tasks and your team entered, you can begin making sense of the steps needed and the order in which they need to be completed. I also add a few milestones, indicated by the black diamond. I put a black diamond for the rollout and set Upgrade Accounting System as a predecessor. This pushes all tasks back so I can see how far out I really need to start. Also notice that after ordering the server, I put in a two-week lead time and a milestone for when I have to have the server here for the upgrade. The order in which things need to be done is as easy as dragging one blue bar to another.

6. Organize workflow using the Gantt chart.

Using the Gantt chart also makes scheduling easy. Tasks that must be done in order can be managed by dragging the time block of the first task to the next and so on. You can drag one task to many and many to one, or a combination of both depending on the need.

Project will configure timing based on the estimated time for each task as well as the Schedule From date. If you're using Schedule From Project Start Date, Project will show you how far out the project will run. Likewise, if you use Schedule From Project Finish Date, Project will tell you the latest you can start and still hit the expected deadline. You can also balance workload. Normally, you have tasks that can be completed simultaneously. When you first enter them in Project, they tend to pile up in the same time frame. After setting the order of related tasks, you can easily see openings in the schedule for other tasks.

7. & 8. Add tasks after the fact and balance the workload

Along with tracking dates, tracking labor resources and balancing the workload are critical parts of any project. The two tasks are also related. Project's resource graph helps track the workload of project members and highlights members who may be underworked or overworked.

When scheduling with the Gantt chart, you may have to stack several tasks that all require time from an individual. Depending on the loading (percentage of time of the task by a person) and length (time required), you may identify an individual who has 16 hours of work per day—obviously not a practical idea. A quick check of the resource graph will let you know when someone is overscheduled or under-scheduled.

Because my projects are smaller in nature than those in most large corporate environments, I really only use this feature to spot-check the plan. This feature will be more useful in evening the load in a larger corporate environment where a number of people can perform the same job functions.

9. Hit the mark.

From the moment a project is approved, the worries set in for everyone involved. Can the project be completed in time? How long will the project take? Use the schedule functionality to ease these worries.

How you set up the time calculations in Microsoft Project depends on the Schedule From option you choose in the project information dialog box.

Use the Schedule From The Project Start Date option for projects that must start immediately and be finished ASAP.

Choose the Schedule Backwards option to start with the finish date for projects that can be launched at any time but must be completed by a designated date.

10. The more you do, the more you learn.

As with any application, the more you work with it, the more comfortable and efficient you become with it. And just like most Microsoft applications, there are plenty of online resources to help. Here are just a few handy links:

- **Microsoft Project Users Group (MPUG-Global)**
  http://www.mpug.org/
  This is the official international community (with over 2,100 members and 30 chapters worldwide) supporting Microsoft Project. The organization serves as an ongoing resource for members to improve their understanding of Microsoft Project and to help maintain their investment in the tool.

- **How-to articles**
  http://search.office.microsoft.com/assistance/tasks.aspx?p=Project
  This comprehensive resource at Microsoft's Project site covers everything from collaboration to formatting issues.
- **Microsoft Project newsgroups**
  http://communities.microsoft.com/newsgroups/default.asp?icp=prod_office&slcid=us
  As TechRepublic members know, the best and most useful advice often comes from users themselves, as demonstrated in these Project newsgroups.
- **Template Gallery**
  http://search.officeupdate.microsoft.com/TemplateGallery/
  You can save time when you can grab a setup that fits your needs. These templates should provide helpful shortcuts for new users.

10 easy ways to turn a dull Word table into a design element

By Jody Gilbert

By default, inserting a table into a Word document gets you a grid. Which is fine. At least Word isn't second-guessing you and applying its own format or foisting some overbearing wizard on you. And if you're after structure rather than design, that grid is all you need. But when you want to move beyond utility and create an attractive element on the page, you need to know a few formatting tricks.

Word comes well supplied with features for jazzing up tables—maybe too many, in fact, empowering users to produce some fairly hideous results. Other users steer clear of table formatting completely after a few failed attempts to put a border where they want it or change a column width without disrupting the table dimensions. Here are a few simple techniques that will enable your users to quickly improve the appearance of their tables without going overboard or wasting time with confusing options.

1. Align the table on the page.

Even if you keep the table formatting simple, its placement can make or break the overall page layout. The simplest positioning trick involves horizontal alignment: left, center, or right. And the easiest way to manipulate the alignment is to select the table (Table | Select | Table) and click the appropriate button (Align Left, Center, Align Right) on the Formatting toolbar, just as you would do to align regular text. Or use the keyboard shortcuts: [Ctrl]L, [Ctrl]E, [Ctrl]R. (The Table Properties dialog box offers the same options, but this way is quicker.) The key here is to make sure the whole table is selected. If only certain cells are selected, these options will apply to the text inside those cells rather than to the table.

2. Wrap text around the table.

In the old days, you had to put a table inside a frame to have text wrap around it. The process is much easier now: Choose Print Layout from the View menu and click on the table to display its move handle. Then, click on the handle and drag the table wherever you want it on the page. This type of layout can make the page more interesting and less linear in design. It can also save on space.

3. Add space around the table.

Once you've dragged a table to a good spot on the page ("good" means the table isn't throwing things off balance by hanging awkwardly into a margin, sitting too high or low, or creating any funky line breaks in the text), you can polish it up by adding some space around it. A little breathing room will enhance readability and reduce that crowded look.

Click within the table and go to Table | Table Properties. In the Table tab, you'll see that the Around option is selected under Alignment. Click Positioning to access the available options. Word is already providing a little space to the left and right of the table (0.13"), but you can increase or decrease that amount if you want. You can also use the Top and Bottom options to add space above and below your table.

4. Add space within the table.

In addition to providing space around the table perimeter, it's a good idea to add some space within the cells. Nothing looks more slapdash than text crammed into a table, which is what you get unless you tweak it a little bit. You have a couple of methods to choose from here.

The first approach is to manually format the text within the cell. Start by clicking within the paragraph you want to format (or selecting multiple paragraphs) and choosing Format | Paragraph. In the Paragraph dialog box, set the desired right and left margins (which will add space on each side of the text within the cell). Then, specify a Space Before and Space After setting. Even 2 or 3 points will improve the appearance of the table text. The advantage of adding space this way is that you can do it selectively, so you have granular control over text positioning in the table.

The second method is to build the extra internal space into the table itself—probably quicker, but your specifications will apply to all the text in the table. Click within the table and choose Table | Properties. In the Table tab, click Options to open the dialog box. Now, just enter the desired measurements in the Default Cell Margins fields.

5. Add space between cells.

Another technique to explore is cell spacing. It's certainly not an essential step for creating an attractive table, but it creates an eye-catching effect, especially if you combine it with shading features. To add cell spacing, click in the table and go back to the Table Options dialog box (Table | Properties | Table tab | Options). Click Allow Spacing Between Cells and then enter the amount of space you want. We're getting into trial-and-error territory now, and you'll need to experiment to see what works best.

6. Turn off gridlines to see where your actual borders are.

One thing that's initially confusing is the difference between the table gridlines (which are a mere visual guide; they don't print) and borders. Working with gridlines turned on is helpful as you build and format a table, but to see what you've produced, choose Hide Gridlines from the Table menu. (You can turn gridlines back on via the Show Gridlines command.) For instance, we removed all the borders from a table and then selectively applied a border to the bottom of the two cells representing signature lines. Turning off gridlines shows whether those borders are formatted properly for the job they're supposed to do.

7. Turn text sideways.

So far, we haven't used the Tables And Borders toolbar, but it offers quick access to some useful options, and we're going to use it now. To display it, just right-click on any visible toolbar and select Tables And Borders from the list of toolbar choices.

The sideways text technique isn't appropriate for all situations, but it's handy to know about it. To rotate your text, select the cell(s) that contain it and click the Change Text Direction button on the Tables And Borders toolbar twice. The first click will rotate the text to the right, which isn't so great for readability. The second click will rotate it so that it runs from bottom to top, like in figures.

8. Manually apply shading and borders.

If you want to add a little color or definition to a table, shading and borders are the way to go. The trick is to make sure you're applying them to the right table components. Although the Tables And Borders toolbar offers a palette of border placement options and lets you "draw" borders of various formats, the Borders And Shading dialog box is probably a little less confusing to use. For applying shading, the Tables And Borders toolbar works okay, but the Borders And Shading dialog box offers more options, so that's what we'll use here.

To demonstrate the process, let's say you want to add a border to the top and bottom of a row and apply a light yellow fill color. Start by selecting the row and going to Format | Borders And Shading. In the Borders tab, you'll see a little image of a table cell with a border on all sides. (This is assuming you haven't changed any border settings; by default, Word tables are formatted with a grid border.) Since you selected a group of cells (a row, actually), Word will set the Apply To dropdown list to Cell (meaning all the cells in the selection). This is what we want, but bear in mind that you can change this to apply to text or to the entire table.

To create the border, click on the left, middle, and right sides of the image to remove those segments, leaving just the top and bottom borders in place. You can make selections from the Style, Color, and Width list boxes if you want. If you do, you'll need to click on the table cell image to apply those selections to the desired sides. To add color, click the Shading tab and click in the light yellow square in the palette of options under Fill.

9. Find your favorite Table AutoFormat styles (and tweak them, if necessary).

Word offers 45 AutoFormat styles—prefab sets of formatting that automatically apply various text and table effects. To see what's available, click in your table and choose Table | AutoFormat (or click the corresponding button on the Tables And Borders toolbar, since we have it displayed now). You can spin through the selections and try them out, see what you like. One of the options is Table Normal, which is handy for those occasions when you want to strip all the formatting from a table (like if you get a little carried away with various embellishments and you're embarrassed to even look at them).

It's important to note that when you apply an AutoFormat style to a table, its specifications will override any formatting you applied to the table yourself. For example, if you set cell margins to add space around the text in the table, you'll lose that if you apply Table AutoFormat because that formatting isn't part of those prefab styles. So apply the AutoFormat style first and *then* set your cell margins.

The AutoFormat choices are handy, and you may just want to use them as is. But you also have a great deal of control over modifying them. For one thing, you'll notice the Apply Special Formats To options at the bottom of the dialog box. If you like everything about a particular style but you want to leave the top row alone, deselect Heading Rows. You may also want to use a style as a starting point and then click Modify. You can do just about anything you want here—it's like modifying a character or paragraph style, only the choices are table-specific.

One final note about Table AutoFormat: If there's a style you want to use all the time, you can select it and click Default. Word will let you set it as the default style for the current document or for the current template.

10. Create a custom table style for instant formatting.

You can use Table AutoFormat to create your own set of attributes and save them as a user-defined style. You can then apply the style whenever you want to create that particular effect. To build a style, open the Table AutoFormat dialog box and click New. Enter a name for the style and choose the existing style that you want to base your new style on. (Word defaults to Table Normal, which is unformatted, in case you want to start with a blank slate.) Make the formatting selections you want for the style. If you want the style to be available to other documents based on the current template, click Add To Template. Otherwise, the style will belong to the current document only. Click OK and then click Close.

To apply the style, click in a table and open the Table AutoFormat dialog box. Choose User-Defined Table Styles from the Category dropdown list box to display your custom style(s). Select the style and click Apply. ❖

10 things you should know about Internet Explorer 7.0 enhancements

By Debra Littlejohn Shinder, MCSE, MVP

Microsoft has made many changes to Internet Explorer that will improve both the user browsing experience and security. The next generation of IE will be included in Windows Vista, but you don't have to upgrade the operating system to enjoy its benefits. Although some IE features will be available only with the Vista version, a version of IE 7.0 will also be available to run on Windows XP with Service Pack 2. This article discusses some of the new features that will make IE 7.0 better and more secure.

1. Tabbed browsing

Users asked for it and now they're going to get it—tabbed browsing, that is. It's a feature made popular by Mozilla Firefox, Opera, MyIE2, and other third-party browsers, and it allows you to view multiple pages with "tabs" in the same browser window so you can switch back and forth between them quickly and easily instead of having numerous browser windows open. You simply click on a tab to view a different open Web page. Because IE was originally designed as a single-window browser and because IE shares code with Windows Explorer, the addition of tabbing to IE was a challenge. However, Microsoft has done it in such a way as to overcome these problems and also retain compatibility with most third-party add-ons. Because the tabbing implementation is multithreaded and each tab uses a separate thread, users will experience faster performance.

2. No phishing allowed

Phishing often involves directing users, via e-mailed links, to fraudulent Web sites (for example, a site that purports to be that of the user's bank but is really the site of a con artist who uses it to collect bank logon credentials). It has become a major threat to Web users.

IE 7.0 contains a phishing filter that can automatically check the sites you visit against a list of known phishing sites, warn you if it is a reported phishing site, and automatically take you away from the site. The browser can also detect that a site uses common phishing tactics even though it hasn't been reported and will display a different alert. A mechanism is included that allows users to easily report phishing sites they discover, to be checked out by Microsoft and added to the list if they're found to be conducting phishing activities.

If you wish, you can configure the browser not to check sites automatically. You can still manually check a specific site that you suspect may be a phishing site.

3. Clear your tracks

Privacy is a big concern, with identity theft on the rise. Many users share computers with others at work or at home, and/or use public computers such as those at libraries and Internet cafés. They want to be able to quickly clear any personal information they've entered in browser forms and get rid of the records of what sites they've visited. In previous browser versions, this requires multiple steps to clear history, temp files, cookies, and so forth.

IE 7.0 simplifies the process with its Clear Tracks option, which is implemented as a top-level menu item. This feature deletes the index.dat files that contain browsing records. Users will no longer need to buy third-party privacy protection software to easily clean up browsing history and other "evidence."

4. Protected mode (low rights IE)

IE 7.0 runs in protected mode, which in early implementations was referred to as low rights IE. This is one of the most important new security features, but unfortunately, you have to run IE 7.0 on Windows Vista to take advantage of it. The feature works in conjunction with Vista's User Account Protection (UAP), which is a philosophy as much as a technology. Simply stated, it runs everything with least privilege by default.

IE protected mode gives the browser only the permissions that are absolutely necessary and also runs add-ons and plug-ins with the lowest possible permissions. Processes run at one of three integrity levels: high, medium, or low. There's no way for a process running at a low level to send data to a higher level process, thus preventing unauthorized elevation of privileges (a favorite trick of hackers).

5. Add-on free mode

Another new mode makes it much easier to troubleshoot problems with IE. Originally called safe mode but renamed add-on free mode, it allows you to boot IE without any plug-ins or extensions. In previous versions, you often ran into problems if, for example, spyware or other malware rendered IE unusable. You needed to download and run an antipyware program to fix it, but the catch-22 was that you couldn't download anything because you couldn't open IE.

Add-on free mode will fix this, allowing you to bypass the extension that's causing the problem and run IE without add-ons in much the same way that you can boot Windows into safe mode and run it without loading drivers that may be keeping you from booting the operating system normally.

6. Opt-in for ActiveX

ActiveX controls allow Web developers to make Web pages much more sophisticated by running miniature applications (similarly to Java applets) that can add high-level interactivity for Web site visitors. However, ActiveX can be exploited to download viruses or Trojans to users' machines and perform other harmful actions, so it can create a security risk.

IE 7.0 attempts to ensure that controls can run only if they're safe to run in the browser. It maintains a database of controls that are intended to run in the browser and checks this list before running an ActiveX control. If the control isn't on the list, the browser will display a prompt to allow the user to opt in (or not) for that control to run in IE.

7. Cross-domain protection and consolidated URL class

A common type of browser attack uses something called cross-domain scripting to redirect browser frames opened in one security domain to a different security domain. IE 7.0 protects against this by making scripts and other objects retain their security context regardless of whether they're redirected. This means, for example, a would-be attacker from the Internet won't be able to run a script in the local machine zone where he would have the permissions of the currently logged on user. Another method of attack exploits the browser's handling of special characters in the URL.

8. Zones lockdown

Internet Explorer has long used the concept of security zones to allow you to implement different security settings depending on whether the site you're accessing is on your local computer, an intranet on the LAN, or the Internet. Zones also make it easy to build a list of sites you trust and other sites that should be restricted. Security templates in previous versions of IE (Low, Medium-Low, Medium, and High) can be used, or you can customize the individual security settings for each zone. IE 7.0 adds a new template, Medium High, for more granular control without having to customize. This template is available when you run IE 7.0 on Vista with protected mode turned on. Other changes include:

- The Intranet zone is disabled by default for most home and small business computers (those that aren't members of a Windows domain).
- The default settings for the Trusted Sites zone provide higher security.
- The slider bars will no longer allow you to select Low or Medium Low security; they only go down to Medium. You can set a zone to lower security by using the custom settings.

9. SSL and TLS

Secure Sockets Layer (SSL) is a standard for encrypting data exchanged between a Web browser and Web server. It's based on public key cryptography and digital certificates to validate the identities of the machines involved in the transaction (server only or client and server).

If there's a problem with a secure site in IE 6.0, the user has to decide what to do. IE 7.0 defaults to the most secure choice. If there's a problem with a certificate, you get a page that explains the problem. Sites are blocked if the certificate has expired or been revoked, if it was issued by an untrusted root certification authority, or if it was issued to a different hostname from the one in the site's URL. Users can still click through the warnings and visit the site anyway unless the certificate was revoked, but they'll get constant warnings.

One warning you won't see anymore (to the relief of many users) is the one that says *this page contains both secure and non-secure items*. Instead, only the secure content will be displayed, and if you want to see the nonsecure content, you can use the Information Bar to unblock it.

Transport Layer Security (TLS) is the successor to SSL and is more secure. IE 6.0 supports SSL versions 2.0 and 3.0, which are enabled by default, and TLS, which has to be explicitly enabled. In IE 7.0, SSL 2.0 (the least secure version) is disabled by default and TLS is enabled.

10. Secure authentication

IE supports various authentication schemes used by Web servers, including basic, digest, integrated Windows authentication, and client certificate mapping. Some of these are more secure than others. For example, basic authentication sends the password as plain text, making it nonsecure unless it's used in combination with SSL/TLS.

Previously, the browser would use the first authentication scheme offered by the server. IE 7.0 corrects this by defaulting to the strongest authentication scheme that's supported by the Web server. It also displays a warning for basic authentication over HTTP, telling the user that the password will be sent in clear text. ❖

3 Windows Server 2003

10 things you should know about Microsoft Windows Server Update Services (WSUS)

By Scott Lowe

In June 2005, Microsoft released Windows Server Update Services (WSUS), the much-anticipated update to its Software Update Services (SUS). As the successor to SUS, WSUS features improvements in patch delivery, status reporting, network usage and implementation, and administration flexibility. The following list outlines ten things about WSUS every network administrator and help desk technician should know.

1. WSUS updates more than just Windows.

SUS, the predecessor for WSUS, was able to keep Windows 2000 SP2 or later, Windows XP Professional, and Windows Server 2003 current with updates. WSUS manages updates for many more Microsoft products. The initial WSUS release will update Windows 2000 and later Windows versions, Office XP & 2003, Exchange Server 2003, and SQL Server 2000, including the desktop edition and MSDE 2000. Microsoft intends for WSUS to eventually handle all Microsoft product updates.

2. WSUS client and server systems require specific hardware and software setups.

WSUS server components run on Windows 2000 SP4 or Windows Server 2003 and require the .NET Framework 1.1 SP1, IIS, MSDE (included with the WSUS download) or SQL Server 2000 SP3a+, IE 6 SP1+, the Background Intelligent Transfer Services 2.0 (BITS) and WinHTTP 5.1. On the client side, Windows 2000 SP3+, Windows XP, or Windows Server 2003 are required. On the hardware side, Microsoft recommends a 1GHz or faster processor and 1GB of RAM for systems that will update 500 or fewer clients, a 3GHz or faster processor and 1GB of RAM for systems that will updated 500 to 10,000 clients, and dual processors with 1GB of RAM for systems that will update more than 10,000 clients.

3. WSUS lacks some of the features found in Microsoft Systems Management Server (SMS).

SMS and WSUS have much in common and will both patch servers and desktop systems. WSUS, however, lacks SMS's ability to deploy and manage systems beyond patching. SMS offers additional capabilities, such as inventory management, advanced reporting, and remote administration.

4. Bandwidth allocation is better with BITS.

WSUS and Windows Update download client updates through the Background Intelligent Transfer Services (BITS) 2.0. BITS uses available bandwidth to download updates in the background. BITS can download large updates and survive network disconnections and other problems. This is an improvement over previous update mechanisms that, during large update downloads, could degrade overall network performance for all users. While it's not a perfect solution to the bandwidth allocation problem, BITS does make an effort to keep update traffic in the background.

5. WSUS has reporting capabilities.

SUS lacked a decent reporting function. Microsoft corrected this oversight by giving WSUS significant reporting capabilities. WSUS's patch status reports will help you identify machines that need patches and could pose a security risk. Other standard reports provide an overall look at WSUS's configuration settings, client update compliance status for an individual update or for an individual computer, or the overall status of each computer using WSUS.

6. WSUS can handle updates in multiple ways.

WSUS clients can download full updates from your WSUS server or directly from Microsoft's update servers. Downloading updates from a local WSUS server provides the best performance when clients are connect to the WSUS server via a dedicated, high-speed network. For locations with limited connectivity to your WSUS server, clients can download updates directly from Microsoft's servers.

7. You control update deployment via server-side or client-side targeting.

WSUS lets you target your updates using machine groups created via two different methods: server-side targeting or client-side targeting. To use server-side targeting, you create and define groups from the WSUS console's Computers tab. With client-side targeting, you assign to groups either through Group Policy or via registry modifications. To create a new group in the WSUS console, choose Computers | Create a computer group, provide a new name, and click OK.

8. WSUS includes command-line capabilities.

The wsusutil.exe program includes command-line options that allow you to import and export update metadata, migrate update approvals from a SUS server to WSUS, and list and remove inactive approvals. Wsusutil.exe is, by default, located at C:\Program Files\Update Services\Tools on your WSUS server. Type *C:\Program Files\Update Services\Tools\wsusutil /?* for assistance with WSUS' command-line parameters.

9. WSUS is scalable.

Even though a single WSUS server can support a great number of clients (more than 10,000), Microsoft built further scalability into the product through "upstream" and "downstream" servers. A "downstream" WSUS server gets its updates from the next server "upstream." Eventually, one of the servers in this chain gets its updates directly from Microsoft Update. WSUS also supports the concept of replicas where multiple servers can mirror most of the settings from a master WSUS server, providing a more distributed update topology.

10. WSUS requires the latest Automatic Update client.

WSUS requires updates to the way that Automatic Updates are applied to some systems. While WSUS makes every attempt to appropriately update the client's version of Automatic Updates, it's not always successful. An unsuccessful update can prevent clients from appearing in the WSUS console. Microsoft created a guide that helps you correct common client update problems. The guide can be found at the following URL: http://www.microsoft.com/technet/prodtechnol/windowsserver2003/library/WSUS/WSUSOperationsGuideTC/b23562a8-1a97-45c0-833e-084cd463d037.mspx. ❖

10 things you should know about Active Directory domain trusts

By Rick Vanover

Domain trusts can be complicated to administer, and it's important to implement changes correctly the first time. Here are some key points to keep in mind to help ensure that your trusts are configured effectively with a minimum of headaches.

1. Determine what kind of trust you should use.

Before deploying a domain trust, you should ensure that the type(s) used are correct for the tasks at hand. Consider the following dimensions of a trust:

- **Type:** Identifies the types of domains involved in trust(s).
- **Transitivity:** Determines whether one trust can let a trusted domain pass through to a third domain.
- **Direction:** Identifies the direction of access and trust (trusted accounts and trusting resources).

Type	Transitivity	Direction
Parent and Child	Transitive	2-way
Tree-root	Transitive	2-way
External	Nontransitive	1-way OR 2-way
Realm	Transitive or Nontransitive	1-way OR 2-way
Forest	Transitive	1-way OR 2-way
Shortcut	Transitive	1-way OR 2-way

2. Get familiar with the Active Directory Domains And Trusts Console.

Trust relationships are managed via the Active Directory Domains And Trusts Console. It lets you perform these basic tasks:

- Raise domain functional level
- Raise forest functional level
- Add UPN suffixes
- Manage domain trust
- Manage forest trust

3. Know the tools.

As with most other elements of the Windows Server family, command-line tools can be used to script repetitive tasks or to ensure consistency in the case of trust creation. Some of the top tools include:

- **NETDOM:** Used to establish or break trust types.
- **NETDIAG:** The output of this tool can give basic status on trust relationships.
- **NLTEST:** Can be used to verify a trust relationship.

You can also use Windows Explorer to view membership to shared resources as they are assigned from trusted domains and/or forests. Active Directory Users And Computers can also provide membership details of Active Directory Objects that have members from trusted domains and/or forests.

4. Set up a test environment.

Depending on your environment and usage requirements, a simple mishap in the creation of domain trusts can have enterprise-wide repercussions. But it's difficult to set up a completely similar test environment to replicate multi-domain and forest issues. Having similar domain scenarios is easier to facilitate, as a means to reinforce the principles and test basic functionality. Consider also template Active Directory objects to test on the live domain relationships to ensure that the desired functionality is obtained but not exceeded before using live groups, accounts, and other objects.

5. Review privileges.

When trusts are created, it's important to ensure that the desired functionality is achieved. But be sure to review the configured trust to verify that the direction of access is correct. For example, if domain A needs to access only a limited amount of resources on domain B, a two-way trust would suffice. However, an administrator from domain B may be able to assign access to resources on domain A. Ensuring the desired direction, type, and transititivity of trusts is critical.

6. Map out the trusts.

Create a map of trusts with simple arrows and boxes illustrating which domains will be trusting and trusted and which trusts will be 1-way and 2-way. Then, with the simple picture(s) in place, map out which domains will trust which—and determine the transititivity as well. This simple chart will make more sense of the greater task at hand and allow you to determine which domains need direction of access and in which direction. Some domains will simply act as a gateway for transitive access to other domains.

7. Document trust relationships.

As organizations marry (and divorce) in today's business world, it's important to have clear documentation of the trust inventory—and to make sure it's accessible without the trust or domain. For example, if you're in Domain B and your headquarters in Domain A sells your division and breaks your trust, your concise documentation saved on a server in Domain A does you little good. Document the type of trust, transitivity, direction, business need for the trust, anticipated duration of the trust, credentials, domain/forest principal information (name, DNS, IP addresses, locations, computer names, etc.), and contact person(s) for the corresponding domains.

8. Avoid making trust relationships too deep.

In the interest of everyone's time, don't nest membership more than one deep when using trusts in multiple domains and forests. Nesting membership can consolidate the number of manageable Active Directory objects, but determining actual membership administration is greatly increased.

9. Know how to manage different versions of Windows.

When running in Windows 2000 and Windows Server 2003 native mode for Active Directory, full functionality is maintained for member domains and forests. If any NT domains or member systems are present in the enterprise, their trust entry functionality is limited by the inability to recognize the Active Directory objects. A frequent strategy in this scenario is to have "domain islands" of those that don't connect to the more common enterprise infrastructure.

10. Remove expired or overlapping trusts.

Changes in business organization may have left unused trusts in place on your domain. Clear out any trusts that are not actively being used. You should also ensure that the trusts you have are set up correctly for the required access and usage patterns. An audit of your trust inventory can be a strong supplement to your well-rounded security policy. ❖

10 things you should know about Microsoft's Enterprise Services

By Scott Robinson

Enterprise Services is one of those Microsoft products whose identity is murky at best. Like SharePoint Services (http://techrepublic.com.com/5138-7343-5806974.html), InfoPath (http://techrepublic.com.com/5138-7343-5800127.html) and other Microsoft software that doesn't seem entirely focused on a single mission, Enterprise Services tends to get lost in the crowd. Whispers that it is nothing more than warmed-over COM+ don't help. And the serious lack of useful documentation almost serves to give it a reputation as something to avoid.

On the other hand, if you're stuck in client-server space and don't have the budget for the heavy-duty stuff, Enterprise Services can equip you to take the enterprise plunge. Here are some powerful features and tricks that aren't particularly visible to the naked eye.

1. Abstract the layers of your architecture with loosely coupled events.

Enterprise Services (http://www.microsoft.com/windowsserversystem/overview/benefits/enterpriseservices.mspx) inherits a substantial legacy from COM+, including the ability of serviced components to publish events to the COM+ facility. COM+ takes over the task of connecting events to clients, and a layer of abstraction is born.

Loosely coupled (http://techrepublic.com.com/5100-6329-1051351.html) events (LCEs) in Enterprise Services are key building blocks in your multitiered environment. Traffic between server(s) and client(s)—that is, published events that clients invoke—is driven by event classes registered with COM+, classes that deliver events to subscribing clients. Connections don't need to be managed from the data source, so your data layer is decoupled; events and clients are dynamically coupled, so you have true enterprise connectivity through your application environment.

2. Optimize your applications, using Enterprise Services concurrency and synchronization features.

Enterprise Services synchronization advances the synchronization techniques of COM+, taking you from apartments to activities: synchronization domains that are based on logical threads (http://techrepublic.com.com/5100-3513_11-5764819.html), rather than physical threads. Physical threads instead form chains that comprise a logical thread, called causalities.

Synchronization domains inherit the TNA (thread-neutral apartment) from COM+; activities leverage the TNA feature of leaving a thread that has entered via a method call even after the method call is done, eliminating a thread switch. Overhead is trimmed because nothing changes but a few TNA variables. If your applications use synchronization domain activities heavily, the overhead savings will be considerable and the environmental performance more optimal.

3. Isolation levels can be configured, allowing you to fine-tune system performance.

Maintaining data integrity across transactions is a matter of locking data while it is being used. There are a lot of variables involved in how well this practice works, including the length of time the data is locked, how many users need it, how often it changes, and so on.

This can be controlled through Isolation level. If you're running Enterprise Services on Windows Server 2003 (http://techrepublic.com.com/5048-22-0.html?nodeIds=all&go=GO&nodeIds=all&tag=search&queryType=4&SearchThis=windows+server+2003), you have control of the Isolation level applied to the locking of data through the Isolation property of the transaction attribute. High isolation levels mean higher data integrity but less concurrency; lower isolation levels increase concurrency but also increase risk to data integrity. The best of all worlds is to find a balance that is right for the application.

4. Manage application states.

Enterprise Services enables you to maintain object states in a number of different places, and your design choices in this area can affect your application scalability. Why? Because tracking object state across multiple client calls to an object and then across many objects can add up to a very significant consumption of resources.

In Enterprise Services, you can manage state at the serviced component level or the client application level, by storing state values at that level. How do you choose which level is appropriate? There are many factors: how fast must state be accessed? How often does it change? Is it linked to users, an application, or multiple applications? Are components load-balanced? Is the object transactional? The point is that Enterprise Services allows you to choose.

You can also, if it makes sense, store state values in a database—useful if, for instance, the state of an application must be restored if your system goes down—or in shared properties (through the Shared Property Manager).

5. Leverage Enterprise Services concurrency and synchronization to enhance quality of data access.

The logical thread concept put forth in #3 offers other across-the-board advantages, not the least of which is an overall reduction in lock-out issues—so data issues due to access errors can be dramatically trimmed. Logical threads muster processes into activities, and those processes are actually facilitated by different physical threads. However, activities themselves are cross-context, cross-process, cross-application, and traffic would get worse, not better, if the traditional approach of locking threads was used. Instead, locks are not used on threads, but on activities.

Specifically, an activity assumes a single logical thread, though the synchronization domain itself can encompass many applications, many contexts, many processes, many physical threads—you really can get very creative with it. The restriction of the single logical thread permits you to link the whole thing together and lock it up with a single event, rather than many. If an activity has a lock on a particular object within the domain, then any other activity wanting access to it waits until the causality lock—the lock on the logical thread—is released. One lock, not many, per activity. Object state is therefore no longer a programming concern per se; activities are availed of synchronization objects that a thread locks upon entering. Those synchronization objects are unlocked, and the activity made available to a new logical thread, when the causality lock is released.

6. Reduce code and development time of applications by aliasing components.

If you're running Enterprise Services on Windows Server 2003, there's a neat trick you can do in development that will yield a faster, smaller app: you can alias components, configuring a single physical component implementation lots of times.

In COM+, you might develop a component and use it many times, in different instances—only register and configure it once—so to get multiple uses out of it, you must create multiple versions, each with its own constructor. The result is lots of cutting and pasting of code.

In Enterprise Services (on Server 2003), it's much simpler. Since you don't have to re-implement the component, you're cutting down on code; you're essentially recycling the component implementation, and you're doing it at the binary level, which is faster, cheaper, and better.

7. Distribute and manage components over a network.

Another COM+ legacy that Enterprise Services leverages is .NET Remoting (http://techrepublic.com.com/5254-6257-0.html?forumID=99&threadID=177006&messageID=1807574&id=935599), which allows events to be sent across your network: "Delegates" are created and events that established parameters and handler method return type for a client. The handler method is implemented and registered with the object event, so the object can remain tied to the client through the event.

You can distribute LCEs (see #2) across multiple systems in a couple of different ways.

LCE routing is subscriber-side networking. Subscribers are defined for both the client system and the system handling the LCE traffic, and COM+ routing is used to do event distribution. (As you might guess, this technique can only be used with persistent subscribers.)

Event-class proxies are another way. You can create a proxy that connects to an event class, since event classes are serviced components. This allows you to network between event classes and publishers.

You can also make the publisher-to-subscriber call asynchronous, passing messages to message queues, with serviced component methods invoked via those messages to buffer the system and further decouple components. This technique can be applied with LCEs and event classes.

8. Create services without components.

The serviced component is the star of the Enterprise Services show. The idea is one of those we-enforce-good-design ideas that Microsoft foists upon unsuspecting developers: COM+ is the lightning in the distributed applications bottle, and to leverage COM+, your code has to be registered with component services, via a `ServicedComponent` class—so that your classes are parsed by service.

If you're running Enterprise Services on Windows 2003, however, life is simpler. Services are applied to a component as a matter of course in a service domain; it is a de facto serviced component, without actually inheriting anything from `ServicedComponent`.

9. Manage transactions through attributes.

One of the major reasons to use Enterprise Services is the automation of transactions, to get away from having to manage transactions in code. Enterprise Services allows you to go in a more efficient direction, managing transactions in attributes.

When you manage transactions in code, you create method arguments that pass transactions. In Enterprise Services, you can have transactions generated by the runtime, and control an object in a class with respect to transactions that apply. The Transaction attribute is applied to classes implementing serviced components and allows you to context with respect to a transaction, which components participate in a transaction, when a new transaction is created, and so on.

10. Object-bound components are assumed.

Object context is used to (among other things) control components with respect to threading and accessibility. Enterprise Services facilitates the creation of context-bound components by virtue of their base class (`ServicedComponent`) deriving from the class `System.ContextBoundObject`. You have .NET Remoting context as a matter of course with serviced components. Context simplifies the fine-tuning of components to the process they support, by defining their runtime requirements and compatibilities. ❖

10 things you should know about BizTalk Server 2004

By Scott Robinson

BizTalk Server 2004, Microsoft's third incarnation of its business process integration server, is the one they got right. Integrated with Visual Studio .NET 2003 and leveraging XML as its data transport backbone, BizTalk 2004 is Microsoft's most powerful offering yet as the company persists in making a serious entry into enterprise integration.

The downside is that there is frustratingly little documentation (http://msdn.microsoft.com/library/default.asp?url=/library/en-us/bts_2002/html/), from Redmond or otherwise , on exactly how best to put this latest, greatest BizTalk to work. (And, fair warning, criticisms of this sort of thing are not the least of the things you should know!) On balance, BizTalk is powerful and versatile but in the long run very difficult to use. Here's a heads-up on both the pros and cons.

1. You can interact with your SQL Server databases from within BizTalk.

BizTalk 2004 can communicate with other sources of data via TCP, file folders, HTTP, ftp, and others. It can also communicate directly with SQL Server (http://techrepublic.com.com/5138-9592-5783491.html) and a configurable SQL adapter. Reducing what would otherwise be a multistage process to a single one is very efficient and convenient: BizTalk can select or update SQL tables via existing stored procedures specified in the adapter configuration and will generate easy-to-use and easy-to-map request and response objects for you.

But there's a downside. Each SQL adapter you create for BizTalk is database-specific, very inconvenient when you have a business process you wish to orchestrate that needs to get into more than one database (if, for instance, your databases are customer-specific but your process isn't). It's possible but not simple to create more than one SQL adapter per orchestration, but no getting around the hard-coding of adapter-to-database (another unfortunate example of Microsoft making our design decisions for us). A more dynamic approach would be welcome, and something we can hope for in future versions.

2. You can synchronize business processes with BizTalk.

BizTalk orchestrations permit you to correlate processes, based on available data. As it is common in many business processes to make certain events and decisions contingent upon the arrival of inbound data, you can stagger or make conditional any business-layer decision or process you choose, with the BTS correlation feature.

You can actually make processes that are architecturally asynchronous (for transaction integrity, robustness, scalability, etc.) logically synchronous by leveraging this feature.

3. BizTalk can take over your EDI, out of the box .

BizTalk 2004 ships with a number of canned adapters, including a Base EDI Adapter that offers the fundamental transaction sets (Purchase Order, Invoice, etc.) and mapping utility to replace your existing EDI interfaces or to launch new ones more economically than you otherwise might, making BizTalk an increasingly attractive investment. The process of configuring and deploying an EDI (http://techrepublic.com.com/5100-10878_11-5054935.html) interface using this adapter isn't painless by any means, but it offers you management options for tracking activity with EDI partners. If you're doing industry-specific EDI, such as health care HL7 transactions, there are BizTalk-compatible packages available from Microsoft.

4. You can deploy a BizTalk application as a Web service.

It is possible, and even surprisingly convenient, to create Web services from BizTalk orchestrations (http://techrepublic.com.com/5100-7343_11-5548172.html). The process mapping of a BizTalk orchestration can be deployed as a service transaction, either network-internal or external, simply by running a wizard. Care must be taken to correctly identify and configure the schema representing the data the Web service will receive, but it can actually be easier to create and deploy a Web service using BizTalk than by other, more conventional means (depending on the job the Web service will be doing).

5. You can monitor processes and track business activity.

BizTalk Server 2004's Business Activity Monitor (http://msdn.microsoft.com/library/default.asp?url=/library/en-us/introduction/htm/ebiz_intro_contentroadmap_aymg.asp) is both an engine and a set of tools that can report process status (in real time, if necessary). This information can be handed off to SharePoint Portal Server, and in turn received by applications in the Microsoft Office suite. The usefulness of the metrics that can be extracted by these tools is obvious, and includes partner-specific performance measures, but the unpolished gem in this capability is the capacity to inform users throughout a process chain of new information as it emerges, allowing them to react immediately if necessary.

6. You can create your own adapters.

Need to roll your own adapter? BizTalk permits you to create custom adapters in order to communicate with proprietary external systems, using the same framework employed by BizTalk's built-in adapters. You can adapt to the external system's communication patterns, and you can (if necessary) embed logic required for message handling. You don't need any additional software to accomplish this, apart from BizTalk 2004, the SDK, and Visual Studio 2003 (http://techrepublic.com.com/5100-22-1058825.html). There are sample adapters included that you can use as a guide.

7. You can leverage MSMQ for asynchronous messaging.

MSMQ (http://www.microsoft.com/windows2000/technologies/communications/msmq/default.mspx) is, as they say, the best Microsoft feature you're not using. Few are even aware of this convenient and versatile messaging capability that comes built-in with XP or MS Server 2003. It's an easy and economical way to connect applications asynchronously—and until now, it wasn't BizTalk-friendly. There was MSMQT (http://msdn.microsoft.com/library/default.asp?url=/library/en-us/deploying/htm/ebiz_depl_config_dbrf.asp) (not quite the same thing), but no MSMQ adapter for BizTalk was available, until earlier this year. Now you can download (http://www.microsoft.com/downloads/details.aspx?FamilyID=CBA87D07-7F50-4D7B-A888-388D123F736E&displaylang=en) it for free and use it to create *Receive* and *Send Ports* in BizTalk systems, to communicate with other applications or with remote business partners.

(**A word of warning:** seek out documentation on potential incompatibilities between MSMQT and MSMQ, when used in the same context.)

8. Some of the most commonplace and important functions are obscure.

Since BizTalk is about connecting systems and applications through messaging, it is built on the assumption that messages are coming in and going out of any process. To this end, a BizTalk orchestration typically starts with a *Receive*, and that *Receive* assumes an initial inbound message. Naturally, it wants to type that message to the schema carrying it. And since Microsoft likes to build "do-it-our-way" safeguards into these processes to urge us away from design mistakes, the orchestration won't receive any message that doesn't match the message type specified in the *Receive* block.

You must generate a type schema from a well-formed XML instance, in order to give BizTalk a selectable type for the Receive block. Yet, amazingly, BizTalk doesn't ship with this capability enabled! You have to do it yourself. The software to perform the schema import XDR schemas is enabled out-of-the-box, but you must run two scripts—`InstallWFX.vbs` and `InstallDTD.vbs`, both found in the `SDK\Utilities\Schema Generator` subdirectory of your BizTalk install—in order to enable the import of XML or DTD for the generation of precise schemas that BizTalk can use for typing. And there are many more examples of critical functions not clearly spelled out in documentation or examples. Be on the lookout!

9. BizTalk orchestrations don't always perform as you'd expect them to.

Another friendly warning about BizTalk is that you're likely to be blind-sided by undocumented inconsistencies between the way you expect things to work and the way they work in BizTalk. One such inconsistency is the manner in which BizTalk orchestrations handle XML.

You can't be very deep into XML (http://techrepublic.com.com/5138-3513-5644970.html) manipulation without availing yourself of xPath, an indispensable utility for extracting data from its XML trappings. In most conventional expressions, you can extract data using xPath with an argument including the source instance and the instance xPath (given in Visual Studio.NET's Properties window, when you've clicked on a particular data item in an XML schema). If you try to use the instance path given in Properties inside a BizTalk orchestration, BizTalk gets lost.

They don't bother telling you that, nor is there any formal documentation that shows you how to pull out single, discrete data items within an orchestration (though we should qualify this statement by saying that this xPath failure only occurs some of the time, depending on the structure of the XML schema and the placement of the desired data item). I've seen some informal explanations for this failure, to do with BizTalk's implementation of XLANG (http://www.gotdotnet.com/team/xml_wsspecs/xlang-c/default.htm). Whatever the cause, this is one of a number of bugs in BizTalk that you won't read about and must confront without assistance.

10. Your time cost will be enormous.

If there ever in the history of Microsoft was a product that was hyped through the roof and then thrown upon the sea, it's BizTalk. Originally a Microsoft acquisition that is now well-integrated into Microsoft's family and lovingly nurtured by its caretakers, BizTalk is powerful, well-conceived, and at this point married to the rest of the MS family—but at the expense of correct and thorough documentation. To say that useful BizTalk how-to and real-world labs are scarce is a howling understatement. Buy into BizTalk and you're more or less on your own, bringing it around to your particular applications and environment.

In short, prepare for endless hours of blogging, followed by endless hours of trial-and-error. You'll get plenty of frustrating hints from the BizTalk Server Administration event log, vague exception messages, and precious little real debugging assistance from the Health and Activity Tracking utility. The upside is that once you've learned the quirks and fixes and tricks, you'll feel incredibly empowered. But, oh, what a learning curve! Don't underestimate it. ❖

10 things you should know about Microsoft's SharePoint Services

By Scott Robinson

SharePoint Services (http://techrepublic.com.com/5100-6346-5069312.html) leverages Microsoft's Web-friendly product philosophy alongside its affinity for desktop apps, and does so in a way (as so many Microsoft products do) that just lulls you into going with the flow. Security is piggybacked on infrastructure already in place; the product's ancillary features are simply more convenient and (despite shortcomings) in many cases more economical to just use, since they're there anyway, than more capable alternatives.

We're inclined not to quibble. SharePoint Services (http://www.microsoft.com/windowsserver2003/technologies/sharepoint/default.mspx) gives you a lot of things you may have found yourself wishing for, things you couldn't have because you'd have to go to the trouble of rolling your own or fiddling with your infrastructure in order to achieve them. And some of them might not be immediately apparent: SharePoint Services is touted as a document management system, and there's a built-in problem with that concept, because we all have a pretty fixed and mundane idea of what a document management system is. SharePoint's Web-centric orientation, however, gives it some unexpected punch and may change your thinking. Here are some points to consider.

1. SharePoint extends Exchange Server.

If you're using Exchange Server (http://techrepublic.com.com/5138-1035-5689059.html) to handle your e-mail traffic, SharePoint can greatly simplify distribution. You can create a SharePoint site as a singular point for receiving Exchange traffic and, at a stroke, have de facto distribution of that traffic to a particular group or groups, with all the security and membership built-in. By setting up a public folder for SharePoint in Exchange, Exchange's work is done—SharePoint pulls from the folder and does the work.

2. SharePoint collaboration solutions are scalable.

It's well-publicized by Microsoft that SharePoint Services is essentially a collaborative solution toolkit. Creating sites for team interaction, sharing and managing of project-specific documents and files, testing, and other collaborative functions are a natural application of SharePoint.

A less hyped aspect of SharePoint is that this collaborative utility is highly scalable. What begins as a resource library shared by a team can be readily telescoped out to accommodate the entire organization or an even broader customer community—SharePoint Services can be readily deployed across multiple servers in a server farm, enabling the creation of massive data stores.

3. SharePoint sites are highly customizable.

SharePoint Services comes fully integrated with FrontPage 2003 (http://techrepublic.com.com/5100-22_11-5104024.html), so all of FrontPage's WYSIWYG Web editing tools are available for use in crafting SharePoint sites. (If your organization swims in the deep end, development-wise, all of this comes with ASP.NET, as well—http://techrepublic.com.com/5100-22_11-1058862.html.)

Via FrontPage, you can leverage the utility of Web Parts, modular chunks of code you can re-use in SharePoint sites, to grab live data from a broad range of possible sources (also see #8). You can allow users to control these modules of code by inserting Web Part zones in your sites, enabling sophisticated drag-and-drop controls. You have complete control over style through XSLT, which you can manipulate either directly or through FrontPage—and you can employ conditional formatting if it desired.

4. SharePoint extends InfoPath.

InfoPath 2003 (http://techrepublic.com.com/5138-7343-5800127.html) is Microsoft's desktop application technology for integrated forms management and data transport. InfoPath is a powerful and underrated technology in itself, and both its XML backbone and forms-friendliness mesh well with SharePoint.

Specifically, you'll find it useful to publish InfoPath forms directly to a SharePoint library. In such a library, forms can be stored and (more importantly) shared and are accessible to working teams leveraging SharePoint as a collaborative tool. (The base form is stored in the library header; populated XML result sets make up the library itself.)

And with SharePoint Portal, you can leverage SharePoint Portal Web services to enhance the utility of InfoPath forms for your desktop community, by accessing information in other systems within your organization (or from outside, for that matter) and populating forms with it as needed.

5. Metadata can be used to create dynamically parsed storage systems.

Metadata is critical to the SharePoint Server concept and comes in several flavors. With metadata you can effectively create customized search arguments that permit you to organize information dynamically and to use search criteria from one document library to retrieve information from another.

Put another way, you can forego the traditional hierarchical folders in organizing your document libraries, if it's appropriate. Instead, you can create metadata lookups that can not only be used as organizational keys for documents in one library but can be used as search arguments to locate documents in other libraries. In this way, you can create searchable document pools with effectively dynamic organization, not only searchable but re-organizable without any physical manipulation of the documents themselves.

6. SharePoint can be a data transport mechanism.

SharePoint's primary features include the ability to set up shared distribution points for data from a wide range of sources, moved by different modes of transport (see #1 and #4). But its data transport role doesn't end there. Depending on what your organization's sites contain, content-wise, and the role(s) the sites are playing in your system, you can actually distribute data from server to server by means of SharePoint's site-moving utilities (see #10).

For instance, if you have SharePoint sites deployed internally to represent data in different workflow stages, the SharePoint content databases of those sites can be rotated in a de facto batch process using these utilities (which are command-line programs and therefore scriptable).

7. Use the Task Pane to turn Word libraries into collaborative systems with built-in administration.

SharePoint Services is primarily about document management. Saving Word documents to SharePoint, placing documents in libraries, and checking them in and out are SharePoint's most obvious functions.

But the extension of those functions into shared workspaces is where those features become really empowering, rather than simply utilitarian. You have a Task Pane that ties documents to libraries, and within it lies a number of important features that take you from the simple management of documents to real collaboration and administration. Through the Task Pane, you can:

- Track status and versioning of documents
- Define and track who has site/document access
- Do task monitoring
- Create alerts

You can, of course, save from all Office applications—not just Word—to SharePoint.

8. SharePoint can pull data from external databases and other data sources.

Web Parts and Web Part architecture (available to your SharePoint development by way of FrontPage 2003 or ASP.NET) can become a powerful component of your SharePoint sites. In particular, Data View Web Parts allow you to add views to your sites from a variety of data sources. You can create views specific to your SharePoint sites and link views together. Data sources can be databases, Web services, or any XML source (InfoPath documents, etc.).

9. Leverage Excel for data management.

Exporting data to Excel is well-supported in SharePoint and makes graphing and printing convenient (via the Print with Excel and Chart with Excel options). But it's also possible (and may often be desirable) to export data to Excel just for the sake of manageability. The Excel Export function creates an Excel Web query linking to the original data. In this way, you can create spreadsheets that will accept data and then push that data to SharePoint.

This can be done by generating an Excel spreadsheet, then linking the spreadsheet to SharePoint (by using Export and Link to Excel from a Datasheet Task Pane). Once this is done, data can be entered into the spreadsheet and pushed from the spreadsheet to Excel with the Synchronize List option.

10. Sites and entire site collections can be backed up in a single operation.

The ability to move a site, lock-stock-and-barrel (and even more so a site collection, which includes primary site, sub-sites, and all their contents), should not be underappreciated. Anyone who's migrated sites the hard way knows it can be maddeningly frustrating. SharePoint Services includes two utilities that will greatly reduce the frustration: `STSADM` and `SMIGRATE`.

`SMIGRATE` began life as an upgrade utility, shepherding data from old SharePoint to new. Now it's for backup/restore and for moving sites wholesale. It's a command-line utility, so it's tailor-made for scripting and can simplify the process of moving a site and its contents to the point that it can conceivably be a content distribution tool in some scenarios.

Its weakness is that when a site is moved with the `SMIGRATE` utility, its security settings don't all move with it. Remember to check your settings after a move or restore.

And while `SMIGRATE` will not preserve your security settings, `STSADM` will. This utility will move not only a site but a site collection, and does far more: you can use it to create sites, delete site collections, import templates, and move data. ❖

10 things you should know about Microsoft's InfoPath 2003

By Scott Robinson

It's easy to look at Microsoft's InfoPath 2003 (http://www.microsoft.com/office/infopath/prodinfo/trial.mspx) as a frivolous add-on to Office 2003 (specifically the Enterprise Edition, which includes InfoPath). It's hard to believe that something that seems an extra, dropped into a desktop product suite like a basket of breadsticks at an Italian restaurant, can be a powerful and flexible desktop application tool. Designed for the not-particularly-technical, it does not appear at face value to be particularly powerful—and therefore not particularly useful to the enterprise-minded developer.

But InfoPath (http://techrepublic.com.com/5138-7343-5749506.html) will surprise you, not only with its considerable fundamental capabilities but with the added utility and features beneath the surface. Below is a sampling of powerful capabilities that don't leap out at you from Microsoft's marketing material, but may persuade you of InfoPath's considerable utility and friendliness, not only to desktop applications but as a bridge between desktop, back-end systems, and the Web.

1. InfoPath gives desktop app users ad hoc access to your core database tables.

InfoPath is generally described as a tool for creating forms that can be used at the desktop level to access SQL Server and Access data. So easy to use and flexible is the InfoPath interface, however, that a desktop user can, with little technical acumen, construct and fine-tune database queries of substantial complexity more rapidly than you might imagine. This also makes InfoPath ideal for desktop-level one-shot apps or temporary, multi-user apps requiring database access.

2. XML can be a new storage medium for your desktop applications.

InfoPath is primarily built as a rapid means of accessing SQL Server and Access databases. It moves data in and out of those sources, however, by means of XML, to which SQL Server and Access technology are increasingly friendly. Have you ever considered that XML is a well-structured and highly utilitarian data storage medium in and of itself?

InfoPath offers you the option of creating XML structures (or leveraging existing ones) not only for data transport but for data storage. While this may seem unconventional and would often be inappropriate when working with existing, large-scale sources or even local Access databases, it might prove particularly convenient when storing data retrieved via ad hoc queries that will be used for other purposes.

3. InfoPath 2003 + BizTalk 2004 = desktop enterprise.

InfoPath's XML underpinnings are shared by Microsoft's BizTalk Server 2004 application integration engine, making enterprise-level applications accessible to desktop-level users. You can take an instance of an InfoPath form and generate a BizTalk message type from it, enabling you to pass forms data into BizTalk processes—and vice versa, creating InfoPath forms from BizTalk message type schemas.

You can also leverage BizTalk 2004's Business Activity Monitor for real-time user notifications. BizTalk's Business Activity Monitor engine tracks business processes from start to finish, which is powerful in itself—but BizTalk's natural compatibility with InfoPath allows you to conveniently plug process status information into Office 2003 tools (Excel, Access, etc.) or into an appropriate network distribution chain (via Sharepoint Portal), where users can track it, respond to it, or redirect it as necessary.

4. InfoPath has built-in Web protocol support.

XML is, for all practical purposes, the native tongue of Web services. Increasingly, Microsoft is buying into XML as its data transport method of choice, in keeping with the over-arching philosophy of Web-centric system design. No surprise, then, that InfoPath has Web protocol support embedded.

5. Swap out data sources.

As time passes, forms will change, and so will data sources. While it's not difficult to create new InfoPath forms when necessary, you can preserve existing InfoPath development by extending forms, adding new data sources, or swapping out old ones. With the InfoPath 2003 Toolkit (http://msdn.microsoft.com/office/understanding/infopath/default.aspx) for Visual Studio .NET, you get a set of utilities that enables you to add ADO.NET data sets and exchange XSD sources.

6. Extend database access for InfoPath solutions by deploying as ASP.NET apps.

InfoPath typically resides on client machines where forms are used, but it's possible to offer the functionality of your InfoPath solutions as ASP.NET Web apps. You lose some of the bells and whistles (such as rich-text formatting), but your users can still edit the information in the form.

To learn more about extending InfoPath with ASP.NET, check out MSDN (http://msdn.microsoft.com/office/default.aspx?pull=/library/en-us/odc_ip2003_ta/html/OfficeInfoPathWebServiceASPNET.asp).

7. Attach files to your form data.

Office 2003 SP1 includes a *File Attachment* control for InfoPath. This feature allows users to store and retrieve files along with form data. An attached file can come from the client machine, from a file share, or even from the Web. You can, as a developer, manipulate this control via .NET Framework methods for encoding and decoding.

8. Implement enhanced digital signature support for application security (with SP1).

The Office 2003 SP1 includes security updates for InfoPath. These include enhanced digital signature support, giving you partial signing, co-signing, countersigning, and non-reputable signing options. Users of your forms can sign different parts of a form. Users can also add notes when signing digitally, and users can roll back to earlier incarnations of a form, based on the incidence of previous signatures.

9. Employ managed code.

The InfoPath 2003 Toolkit for Visual Studio .NET lets you move easily between InfoPath and Visual Studio. You can customize InfoPath development with VB.NET or C#, meaning you can implement managed code solutions.

10. Use InfoPath in combination with VS.NET 2003 to implement business logic in simple forms.

Managed code means you can go farther in implementing logic in your forms. The Toolkit, presupposing the presence of `VS.NET 2003`, will insert InfoPath Projects into `Visual Studio | New Project`, and you'll see an InfoPath form icon under VB Projects and C# Projects.

VS.NET will include your InfoPath forms, and the projects for developing them, in the Solution Explorer window. If you've developed a form and wish to extend it via managed code, your event-handling script code can be migrated into the VS.NET project. The script code will be disabled, but the script files are referenced in Solution Explorer: you can usually import your event-handling code into managed-code event handlers with just a little tweaking.

You'll also have access to .NET classes for InfoPath COM object wrappers, enabling you to use delegates for event handlers found in the form designer. This is really convenient, permitting you to rapidly generate event handlers to encapsulate logic. You can also bolster the security of InfoPath applications by embedding validation in event handlers. And with SP1, you have open-ended group and field validation expressions; you can format forms conditionally, modify the execution of an application based on user role, and implement event-based business rules in the application. ❖

10 things you should know about Microsoft's SQL Server 2005

By Scott Robinson

The fanfare from TechEd 2005 (http://techrepublic.com.com/html/blogs/teched2005.html) in June 2005 was vintage Microsoft: lots of happy noise about miraculous products with tongue-in-cheek delivery dates, as many of us suppressed a yawn. But let's give credit where it's due; we've waited a long time for a new SQL Server (http://techrepublic.com.com/1200-10880-5737262.html), and the features Microsoft is delivering with its upgraded database technology are what we've asked for and then some. Here's a rundown on the features we'll find most useful.

1. There is now an XML data type.

If there's any feature of SQL Server 2005 to jump up and down about, it's the new native XML (http://techrepublic.com.com/5100-3513-5805291.html) data type. Why? Apart from the giant leap forward of an already Web-friendly agenda, the new type offers us design options that are atypical of Microsoft, which generally likes to do our designing for us.

The new XML data type:

- Can be used in a table column
- Can be used in a stored procedure, as a parameter or as a variable
- Can store untyped data
- Can check against a schema to see if data stored in a column typed as XML matches that associated schema (if there's no schema, the data is considered untyped)

And the mapping between XML data and relational data is bidirectional.

2. Distributed Management Objects (DMO) becomes SQL Server Management Objects (SMO).

SQL Server Management Objects (SMO) (http://techrepublic.com.com/5100-9592_11-5796703.html) is a .NET Framework-based management framework (http://techrepublic.com.com/5100-3513_11-5782941.html) that lets you create custom applications for server management. SMO (like DMO before it) allows you to handle columns, tables, databases, and servers as objects, programmatically—and SMO supports SQL Server 2005's new features, like Service Broker.

SMOs are optimized, not instantiating objects fully (with all the properties retrieved) until the object is explicitly reference. You can also batch SQL commands and create scripts to create objects.

Your custom server management apps can be used to manage SQL Server 7 in SQL Server 2000 systems as well.

3. Common Table Expresssions (CTEs)—recursive queries.

A common table expression (CTE) enables queries to be recursive. A CTE can be self-referential, with an upper limit on the incursions. You can use the CTE as a part of a WITH and in a SELECT, UPDATE, INSERT, or DELETE command.

4. The Service Broker makes SQL Server traffic asynchronous.

There's a front-end queuing system, and it changes everything. You can now manage SQL Server traffic by rendering it asynchronous with the new Service Broker feature. It enhances scalability by enabling your system to handle more traffic logically that it can handle physically. The Service Broker can be accessed via SQL commands and allows transactions to include queued events.

Those who know me well would never accuse me of being a Microsoft disciple, but this feature impresses me in no small measure and I'm pleased to call attention to it. Adding easily-configured asynchronicity (http://techrepublic.com.com/5100-22_11-5087336.html) to the data layer of an enterprise system is a boon to developers and opens up huge possibilities for Web apps. The economy with which those apps can now scale can't be overstated. Service Broker alone is a reason to consider upgrading to SQL Server 2005.

5. Create .NET triggers.

SQL Server 2005 is .NET-integrated to a promising degree (it has distressed us for some time that Microsoft's commitment to .NET is as hedged as it is), and one useful consequence of this integration is the ability to create user-defined triggers (UDTs) through Visual Studio 2005.

The Trigger option can be pulled from the template list in Visual Studio, generating a file for the code to be triggered. The mechanism tying this code to SQL is a SqlPipe. It's deployed in your Build | Deploy. You can work it in the other direction (i.e., from CLR) by referencing the Trigger object in a T-SQL CREATE TRIGGER command.

6. SQL Server 2005 configuration is dynamic.

If you're running SQL Server 2005 on Windows Server 2003, its configuration is fully dynamic—you can change configuration values on-the-fly without restarting the server and get immediate response (the same is true for Address Windowing Extensions).

7. Define your own data types.

The user-defined type, enabled by the integration of SQL Server 2005 and the .NET CLR, is a consolidation of previous practices, allowing you to create application- or environment-specific types. You can extend more general types into variations that only except values you define—no more triggering or constraints. Validation is built in to the field.

8. Many active result sets, one connection.

This is another feature not just to make note of, but to get excited about. MARS (Multiple Active Result Sets—http://techrepublic.com.com/5100-22_11-5161213.html) enables you to execute multiple queries yielding multiple results, over a single connection. An application can move between open result sets as needed. The performance and scalability benefits are obvious.

This new trick is courtesy of the new ADO.NET, in tandem with SQL Server 2005's ability to accommodate multiple active commands. Since MARS is part SQL Server 2005 and part ADO.NET 2.0, it is only available if you're using both.

9. WAITFOR ... RECEIVE.

In previous versions of SQL, WAITFOR was static. We fed it some wait-time value, and that was what it could do. Now WAITFOR is dynamic; tell it to wait for a RECEIVE statement's results, whenever that might be delivered.

Beyond the usual this-is-cool, we can appreciate this feature because of the manner in which it accommodates the new Service Broker (see #2). Since Service Broker makes database query ability asynchronous via queuing (and therefore extremely dynamic), and a particular database query may sit in a queue for an undetermined period, the new dynamic WAITFOR is ideal for responding to RECEIVE results that will emerge at the discretion of Service Broker.

10. DTS is now Integration Services.

There's a new architecture underlying data transformation. The very popular and widely used DTS is now Integration Services (http://techrepublic.com.com/5100-3513_11-5765005.html) and consists of a Data Transformation Pipeline and a Data Transformation Runtime.

The pipeline connects data source to data target by means of data adapters, with transformations between them. It's a conventional structure, but implemented in such a way as to enable considerable complexity: for instance, you can do one-to-many mappings and create columns with output derived from a transform.

The Data Transformation Runtime gives you components for organizing data loading and transformation processes into production-oriented operations, within which you can manage connections and manipulate variables. It's basically a run-time object framework that can be bundled into managed .NET apps.

DTP and DTR components are used to create Integration Services packages, similar in principle to the familiar DTS packages but with much greater levels of configurability and control, particularly in the area of workflow. ❖

Linux

4

10 things you should do to a new Linux PC before connecting to the Internet

By Kirk R. Halyk

1. Determine your purpose.

Linux, like Microsoft Windows, is simply a computer operating system. When I talk to friends or coworkers who are embarking on the Linux experience for their initial time, this is the first point I stress. Linux in itself is not a magic wand that can be waved and make all sorts of computing problems disappear. While Windows has its own set of problems, so too does Linux. There is no such thing as a perfect or completely secure computer operating system. Will the machine be a desktop computer or a server; purpose is a key to understanding how to initially install and configure your Linux PC.

2. Choose your installation.

Unlike Windows, Linux does not present itself as a "server" version or as a "desktop" version. During a typical installation of Linux the choice is yours as to exactly what software you wish to install and therefore exactly what type of a system you are constructing. Because of this, you need to be aware of the packages that the installation program is installing for you. For example, some distributions will configure and start a Samba server or a mail server as part of the base install. Depending upon the purpose of your Linux PC and the security level you are prepared to accept, these services may not be needed or desired at all. Taking the time to familiarize yourself with your distributions' installer can prevent many headaches and/or reinstalls down the road.

3. Install and configure a software firewall.

A local software firewall can provide a "just in case" layer of security to any type of network. These types of firewalls allow you to filter the network traffic that reaches your PC and are quite similar to the Windows Firewall. The Mandriva package called Shorewall, along with a component of the Linux kernel called *Netfilter*, provides a software firewall. By installing and configuring Shorewall during the installation process, you can restrict or block certain types of network traffic, be it coming to or going out from your PC.

To access and configure your firewall for Mandriva simply run the `mcc` (or Mandriva Control Center) command from a command prompt or, depending upon your graphical environment, you may be able to access the Mandriva Control Center from your base system menu. In the security options, select the firewall icon and you will be presented with a list of common applications that may need access through your firewall. For example, checking the box for SSH Server will open port 22 needed by the Secure Shell server for secure remote access. There is also an advanced section which will allow you to enter some less commonly used ports. For example, entering *8000/tcp* will open port 8000 on your PC to TCP-based network traffic.

Blocking or allowing network traffic is one layer of security, but how do you secure a service that you do allow the Internet or your intranet to connect to? Host-based security is yet another layer.

4. Configure the /etc/hosts.deny and /etc/hosts.allow files.

In the preceding section we looked at the example of opening the Secure Shell service to network traffic by opening port 22 on our firewall. To further secure this server from unwanted traffic or potential hackers, we may wish to limit the hosts or computers that can connect to this server application. The `/etc/hosts.deny` and `/etc/hosts.allow` files allow us to do just that.

When a computer attempts to access a service such as a secure shell server on your new Linux PC the `/etc/hosts.deny` and `/etc/hosts.allow` files will be processed and access will be granted or refused based on some easily configurable rules. Quite often for desktop Linux PCs it is very useful to place the following line in the `/etc/hosts.deny` file:

```
ALL: ALL
```

This will deny access to all services from all hosts. It seems pretty restrictive at first glance, but we then add hosts to the `/etc/hosts.allow` file that will allow us to access services. The following are examples that allow some hosts remote secure shell access:

```
sshd: 192.168.0.1   #allow 192.168.0.1 to access ssh sshd:
  somebox.somedomain.com #allow somebox.somedomain.com to
  access ssh
```

These two files provide powerful host-based filtering methods for your Linux PC.

5. Shut off or remove nonessential services.

Just like Windows there can be services running in the background that you either don't want or don't have a purpose for. By using the Linux command `chkconfig` you can see what services are running and turn them on and off as needed. Services that are not running don't provide security holes for potential hackers and don't take up those precious CPU cycles.

6. Secure your required services

If your new Linux PC has some services that will receive connections from the Internet make sure you understand their configurations and tune them as necessary. For example, if your Linux PC will receive secure shell connections make sure you check the `ssh config` file (for Mandriva it is `/etc/ssh/sshd_config`) and disable options like root login. Every Linux PC has a root user so you should disable root login via `ssh` in order to dissuade brute force password crack attempts against your super-user account.

7. Tune kernel networking security options.

The Linux kernel itself can provide some additional networking security. Familiarize yourself with the options in the /etc/sysctl.conf file and tune them as needed. Options in this file control, for example, what type of network information is logged in your system logs.

8. Connect the PC to a router.

A hardware router is a pretty common piece of household computer hardware these days. This is the frontline security to any home or business network and provides multiple PCs to share one visible or external Internet address. This is generally bad news for any hacker or otherwise malicious program that may take a look at your new Linux PC as it blocks any and all network traffic that you don't specifically allow. Home networking routers are just smaller versions of what the big companies use to separate their corporate infrastructure from the Internet.

9. Update.

Always keep the software on your computer up to date with the latest security patches should you be running Linux, Windows, BSD, or WhoKnowsWhat. Your distribution will release regular security patches that should be applied and are available off the Internet. As with Windows, this should always be your first Internet destination.

10. Install other software.

Your second Internet stop may be to install some other hardening or system monitoring software.

Bastille-Linux (http://www.bastille-linux.org/) is a program that can be used to "harden" or secure certain aspects of your new Linux PC. It interactively develops a security policy that is applied to the system and can produce reports on potential security shortcomings. On top of that it is a great tool to use for learning the ins and outs of securing your Linux PC.

Tripwire (**http://sourceforge.net/projects/tripwire**) is a software package that monitors your system binaries for unauthorized modifications. Often a hacker may modify system binaries that may be useful in detecting a system intrusion. The modified programs would then report false information to you, allowing the hacker to maintain his control over your system. ❖

10 things you should know about every Linux installation and distro

By Jeffrey G. Thomas

Linux (http://techrepublic.com.com/5138-1035-728754.html)is not Windows, and although there are some similarities, you must realize that there may be a few "new ways of doing things" to learn before you can be comfortable in Linux. Linux is an open-source clone of UNIX, a secure operating system (OS) that predates DOS and Windows and is designed for multiple users. The items in the following list generally apply to any UNIX-based *nix system, such as Linux and the various BSDs. For the purposes of this article, assume that it's all Linux.

1. File hierarchy

Unlike some other OSs that have a file tree for each drive, the Linux file system is one big tree. At the top you have / (Root) and every folder, file, and drive branches off of this Root.

For example, say that you have two hard drives (named `a` and `b`), one floppy drive, and one CD-ROM. Let's say that the first hard drive has two partitions (named `a1` and `a2`). In Windows, it would look like this:

```
+ hard drive a, partition one (hda1): C Drive
+ hda2: D Drive
+ hdb1: E Drive
+ floppy: A drive
+ CD-ROM: F Drive
```

In Linux, you have one file system, not the five listed in the Windows example. Each drive is mounted onto the tree and acts just like a folder. The drives could be placed like this:

```
+ hda1: / (our Root)
+ hda2: /home
+ hdb1: /home/user/music
+ floppy: /mnt/floppy
+ CD-ROM: /mnt/cdrom
```

Our D drive and E drive are attached within our C drive and there is no need to go to the top to switch drives; the switching happens seamlessly as we move from one folder to another. The same is true with our Floppy and CD-ROM: they are just attached under `/mnt` as part of the one file system. These drives, in reality, can be attached almost anywhere in a Linux system, depending on how the installation (or user) set up the `/etc/fstab` file, which tells the computer where things get attached and how to handle them.

2. Modular system

Think about the guts of Windows XP, Win2k, Win98, Win95, and Apple OS X. Each has different components inside and a different graphical look. What if you wanted the Media Player in XP, the File Manager in 98, the stability of Win2k, and the look of OS X all in one unit? In Linux, each aspect of the system is independent, so you can mix and match parts to make your very own Frankenstein OS. You can choose from a variety of programs to run as your firewall, another to play media, yet another to run your File Manager.

Unlike the "tower" OS's from Microsoft, where everything is interconnected and depends on each aspect of the system, the Linux OS is spread out like a market: everything works together for the common good, but vendors (independent parts of the OS) can be excluded, and the OS will still function. Don't want a Media Player or File Manager? Take it out! Your OS will not fall like a broken tower.

This modularity is the reason for so many distributions of Linux (commonly called distros); any person or company can mix and match the programs they find most useful and slap a name on that collection. RedHat, Xandros, SimplyMEPIS, and Suse are all examples of distros.

Some of the larger distros have copycats that use their settings, but change the included programs. This is the Linux way, and the mix-and-match approach gives users more choice in the long run. DistroWatch.com currently lists over 350 distributions of Linux. Many on the list are specialized to serve a specific group of people, but all can be altered to run the same programs.

Because programs are interchangeable, the Graphical User Interface (GUI) is no exception. GUI's give you the look and feel of a modern OS with the mouse, program icons, menus, etc. Any Linux system (well, one that is running on a real computer, not a phone) can run one of many different GUIs, just like it can run many Web browsers or different e-mail client programs.

Want your system to look like Windows? Use FVWM with the XP theme. Want it to be fast? Try IceWM. Want it to be more "full featured"? Try GNOME or KDE. All of these GUIs have benefits and drawbacks, but they all present the user with an interface that can be manipulated with a mouse. Although this may result in every Linux screen looking different, all of the GUIs are still doing the same behind-the-scenes work for you; just use your eyes and often it is not hard at all.

3. Hardware, software, and everything in between

Linux has come a long way in the few short years of its existence. It is less than half the age of Microsoft Windows, and yet it is more powerful, more stable, less resource-hungry, and graphically equal (if not superior) to this costly, buggy OS from Redmond.

One thing that Linux doesn't yet have going for it is vendor support. If you really like Intuit's QuickBooks, for example, you cannot natively run it in Linux. There are projects to make Windows programs run in Linux, such as CrossOver Office (http://www.codeweavers.com/) and Wine, but these work with varying success, depending on the Windows program. Until software companies decide to port their programs to Linux, you will not be able to run them natively.

Not all is lost, however. Open Source software has upward of 15,000 programs that run natively in Linux. Because these programs are (usually) free of charge, they vary in quality, but the majority of the programs are wonderfully written and constantly improved. These programs can import and export non-native file types as well. GNUCash can read those Quickbooks files just fine, and OpenOffice.org can read MSWord *.doc files. If you dislike GNUCash, don't despair. There are other similar programs also available for free, and more and more software companies are releasing Linux versions of their software.

These same issues apply to hardware. Just as you cannot expect just any piece of hardware off the shelf to work with an Apple computer, the same can be said for Linux machines. Most standard hardware works perfectly; hard drives, RAM, flash drives, motherboards, NICs, and digital cameras usually have little trouble under Linux. Newer, cutting-edge hardware is a different story. Until hardware vendors choose to support Linux, the drivers needed to work these pieces of hardware must be written by the Linux community for free and in the community members' spare time.

Therefore, there is a lag behind Windows support since hardware companies often work directly with Microsoft to ensure compatibility, and tend to let Linux volunteers figure out the Linux hardware support on their own. Laptops are notorious for their nonstandard hardware; it can be a challenge to map special keys in Linux. The good news here is that vendor support for Linux hardware, like software, is changing for the better as more and more companies see their future in Linux.

Everything in between the hardware and the software in a Linux machine is the kernel. This kernel is what connects the hardware to the software, and an updated kernel is made available via the Internet every few weeks; the most current is 2.6.14. If you have hardware that isn't currently supported, there is a chance that a newer kernel could help you out. Installing this kernel yourself isn't always easy, however; that's where Package Managers come into play.

4. Package Managers—Program installation made easy(er)

There are many ways to install programs in Linux, but the easiest is with your distribution's Package Manager (PM). The PM makes sure that any missing files (called dependencies) are also installed so the program runs correctly. Choosing a distribution often comes down to which type of PM you like, but any Linux software can be installed on different distributions if you can find the corresponding Package.

These PMs usually have an on-line repository for their programs. Installing an application is as easy as searching through the program repository and clicking Install. Can't find `IceWM` or `MPlayer` in your Package Manager's list? There is always a way to add a new on-line repository that will have what you are looking for. Some examples of Package Managers include Synaptic (based on dpkg and Apt) for Debian (and derivatives); Yum for RedHat (and derivatives); YaST2 for SuSE (and derivatives); and Emerge for Gentoo.

5. Permissions

Linux is designed to have multiple users, and these users fall into groups. Every user has permissions to read, write, or execute (R/W/X) their own files, and permission to change those permissions. Because Linux is designed for multiple users, users have their own individual password and may restrict access to their files. These are called User Permissions.

Each user belongs to one or more groups, and a user can set their file/folder permissions so that others in the group can read but not write the files, or any other combination of R/W/X. These are Group permissions. For example, Joe and Susan are both in Accounting. They can allow the Accounting group access to each other's files, but they can restrict that access from those in the Sales group.

The `Others` permissions can allow or deny access to these files for anyone outside the Group. These permissions are for the safety of the overall system, as well as for each user's data. Most home users are fine to leave the default permissions alone on their files.

The Root user (not to be confused with the / Root of a file system), as the Administrator, has rights to all files and is the only user who can alter system-wide settings. The Root user has their own password, which is used for system maintenance. This distinction prevents a regular user from installing harmful spyware on the system or deleting important files.

6. Home directory

Windows has My Documents, but where do you put files that aren't documents? Usually on the Windows Desktop! Linux can clutter the desktop too, but each of our users also has a Home directory, usually located at `/home/user`. Within that Home directory we often have Documents (`/home/user/documents`), program links, music (`/home/user/Music`), or whatever we want. We can create files and folders here, and organize or disorganize them as much as we want, just like it was our own personal Home. Depending on how our permissions are set, we can allow or prevent any other user access to these files (except the Root user).

7. Default installation differences

There are a few differences between Linux distributions, such as where some files are kept or what some of the default programs are named. Just knowing that the file system might be a bit different between RedHat and SuSE is a great start. Most users don't need to know what those differences are, but they should be aware that the internal file systems can be a bit different. When asking for help, make sure to let others know which distribution you are running. If you don't have troubles in your system or don't care to set up complex behind-the-scenes operations, don't worry too much about this.

8. CLI, or "how to run"

From the Start-type menu, the `xterm` program (also called Console) brings you to a Terminal, which looks a bit like a DOS window, but it actually predates and outpowers DOS. This is the Command Line Interface (CLI), the origin of our favorite OS which is present in every Linux distribution. We won't get into the finer details, which can fill books, but the CLI a powerful tool often needed to troubleshoot your computer. If you ask for help on the Internet and someone asks you to run `lspci`, they want you to start `xterm`, type *`lspci`* [enter] and provide the screen's response.

When you start an `xterm`, you are your regular user-self with limited powers. To get into Root User mode (see Permissions above) in an `xterm`, type *`su`* [enter], then the Root password [enter]. Now you have a lot of power so be nice. The Root user can destroy anyone's data, including the system files needed to run Linux. To leave an `xterm` or `su` mode, type *`exit`* [enter].

9. Ctrl-alt-escape

Clicking the ctrl-alt-escape key combination changes your mouse into an X, skull-and-crossbones, or some other sinister mouse-cursor. In this mode, clicking on a misbehaving or frozen application will *`kill`* it. It is similar to the End Process in Windows Task Manager, but use with care. If you don't want to kill anything, use the Esc key to back out of kill mode. Clicking on the wrong program (including the desktop GUI) can cause a serious headache.

10. The Internet is your friend!

Many distros have a User's Forum where questions, answers, and tips are passed around. LinuxQuestions.org is a great site for overall Linux knowledge and help. Remember, before posting questions on any forum, research your questions (both at LQ and on Google) to avoid asking about an issue that may already be solved. Also, check the age of any solution that you find, as old answers may no longer apply to this fast-changing world of Open Source software. When asking a question, be sure to include as much (applicable) information as you can about your system, such as:

- The processor type (Intel or AMD or Apple PPC?)
- Your distribution (SuSE? Debian?)
- The program with which you're having trouble
- Any other relevant information.

Keep an open mind

Linux and open-source software have made leaps and bounds in the last few years, but for users coming from the closed world of Windows, the internal workings of Linux may seem foreign. An open mind and a willingness to share knowledge helps the Linux community grow, and we welcome you to our ranks. ❖

10 things you should do to prepare every new Linux installation

By ipkernel

1. Install latest patches.

There are over 200 different Linux distributions, and you will need the patches that are specific to your distribution. Search for needed patches on the Web site of your distribution maintainer (example: Debian (http://www.debian.org/), Redhat (http://www.redhat.com/), Lindows (http://www.lindows.com/), etc.). Other sources for updated software are Freshmeat (http://freshmeat.net/), Ibiblio (http://www.ibiblio.org/pub/Linux/), and Linuxberg (http://www.linuxberg.com/). Some systems use package managers, such as *rpm* (Red Hat Package Manager) or *deb* (Debian Package Manager), while others will require a little more effort. These links should provide access to updated software as well as pretty clear instructions for installation. Be sure to read the documentation since there may be dependencies that will need to be satisfied to ensure a smooth update.

2. Create and configure user accounts.

Even if you are the sole user of your system, you still need to create a user account for normal usage. The Root, or super user, account should only be used when absolutely necessary. This improves system security and reduces the possibility of accidentally corrupting portions of the system that would render it unstable.

Most Linux distributions come with an Admin tool that can be used to create and configure user accounts. This is the best way to proceed since it will lower the possibility of typographical or other errors that could cause problems. If you will have multiple users, creation can be simplified by first configuring the Default User.

You should require that all users have secure passwords, at least eight characters long, with multiple types of characters. Do not use words as part of the password since this just makes it easier for potential hackers. Enable shadow passwords so the passwords will not be stored on the system in clear text. Any daemon or service account that does not require shell access should be modified by using the `chsh` command to change its shell assignment to */bin/false*. This will prevent hackers from using default system accounts to log in to the machine.

You should also ensure that no accounts other than Root have a user ID of zero, and you should prevent remote login access without passwords by not allowing `.rhost or /etc/host.equiv` files.

3. Secure Root access.

Securing Root, also known as Super User, is the single most important action you must take to secure your system. After ensuring you have another user account you can use to log in to the system, it is good to disable Root login capability. Thus, you would log in with standard user access, and when you needed the administrative capability of Root you could access it temporarily with the *su* command. Direct login by Root can be prevented in most distributions by editing the file `/etc/security` so there is a hash (#) at the beginning of each line. As part of this step you should:

- Ensure the telnet server package is not installed so telnet access is unavailable.
- Prevent `SSH` login by editing the file `/etc/ssh/sshd_config`. For example, in Red Hat you would change the `DenyUsers` line to read `DenyUsers root`.
- Limit Root's search path to only those directories needed for administrative tasks. Check Root's `.cshrc`, `.login`, and `.profile` files to ensure the current directory `(.)` is not part of the search path.
- Ensure protection for files created by Root. Set Root's `umask` to 077 (read, write, and execute permissions only for Root) or 022 (other users can read and execute but not change).

4. Secure physical access.

Go into Setup, set a BIOS password, and configure your system to boot from the hard drive only. This will prevent an attacker with physical access from simply loading a bootable disk, recycling power on the system, and gaining root access quite easily. Of course the attacker could still accomplish the same thing by clearing the CMOS, but this does make it less likely.

5. Remove and/or disable unnecessary system services.

The command `ls -l /etc/rc.d/rc3.d/S*` or `ls -l /etc/rc.d/rc5.d/S*` for graphics mode will show startup scripts. You can then verify only necessary services are running and use `chkconfig` to stop a service from loading at startup. An example command would be:

```
/sbin/chkconfig -levels 2345 <service_name> off
```

Where *<service_name>* is the service that should not run and `2345` refers to the run-levels where the command will apply.

Some distributions will need to have services removed from `/etc/xinetd` or `/etc/xinetd.conf`. The service listed in `/etc/xinetd.conf` can be disabled simply by placing a hash mark (#) at the beginning of the line that loads it.

6. Control network access.

Most distributions automatically include TCP wrappers, which may be used to control services based on IP addresses and host names. Edit `/etc/hosts.allow` to read `ALL: LOCAL` to permit local logins and edit `/etc/hosts.deny` to read `ALL: ALL` to deny remote connections. Specific ports may be listed if you need to allow some remote connections.

`IPTABLES` regulate the ports from which packets will be allowed to access your system. Some distributions, including RedHat, automatically configure this based on which system services are specified as required during system installation. Please consult the documentation for your particular distribution to ensure this important "firewall" is enabled.

If you must have FTP enabled, make sure it's as secure as possible. Reference CERT Tech Tips (**http://www.cert.org/tech_tips/**) for instructions on FTP configuration.

7. Configure auditing and system logs.

Log files can be your most important tool in resolving any difficulties that arise. `Syslog` is the daemon that controls the Linux log files and its configuration is controlled by `/etc/syslog.conf`. All log files should be owned by Root.

There is a new generation logging daemon that allows greater sorting capability, thereby making management easier. Review its capabilities at Freshmeat Syslog-ng (**http://freshmeat.net/projects/syslog-ng/**).

Logwatch (**http://www2.logwatch.org:8080/**) or Swatch (**http://swatch.sourceforge.net/**) are well-known, tested, and tried utilities for automatically monitoring log files and alerting you to possible problems.

8. Configure file security.

Only Root should have access to CRON. Otherwise, anyone gaining access to the system could schedule a damaging process to run at any time. Root should be the owner and group for `/etc/fstab`, `/etc/passwd`, `/etc/group`, `/etc/shadow`. Verify the permissions for these files are 644, except for `/etc/shadow`, which should be 400.

9. Prepare for disaster recovery.

Create a boot disk for your newly configured system. Most distributions include the utility `Mkbootdisk` which makes this a simple endeavor.

You should plan to back up important data on a regular basis. To create a `tarball` of a specific list of directories, issue the command:

```
tar -cvf archive-name.tar dir1 dir2 dir3...
```

Where `archive_name.tar` is the name of the tarball you are creating and `dir1`, `dir2`, etc. are the directories being copied to it.

Suggestions for more comprehensive backups may be found at this "HowTo" (http://www.tldp.org/HOWTO/Linux-Complete-Backup-and-Recovery-HOWTO/), and serious fault tolerance can be provided by creating a system image of your ideal load.

10. Plan for system maintenance.

Get yourself added to some mailing lists that will notify you of updates for your Linux distribution. Distribution maintainers usually have a mailing list for notifying users when a new stable distribution or important patches have been released.

Some sites that will alert you of current security issues include:

- LinuxSecurity (http://www.linuxsecurity.com/)
- SANS (http://www.sans.org/)
- CERT (http://www.cert.org/)
- Linux Today (http://e-newsletters.internet.com/linuxtodaysecurity.html/)
- Security Focus (http://www.securityfocus.com/) ❖

10 things you should already know about the Linux bash shell

By Mellonfire

If you've ever typed a command at the Linux shell prompt, you've probably already used bash–after all, it's the default command shell on most modern GNU/Linux distributions. The `bash` shell is the primary interface to the Linux operating system—it accepts, interprets, and executes your commands and provides you with the building blocks for shell scripting and automated task execution.

Bash's unassuming exterior hides some very powerful tools and shortcuts. If you're a heavy user of the command line, these can save you a fair bit of typing. This document outlines ten of the most useful tools.

1. Easily recall previous commands.

Bash keeps track of the commands you execute in a history buffer and allows you to recall previous commands by cycling through them with the Up and Down cursor keys. For even faster recall, "speed search" previously executed commands by typing the first few letters of the command followed by the key combination `Ctrl-R`; bash will then scan the command history for matching commands and display them on the console. Type *Ctrl-R* repeatedly to cycle through the entire list of matching commands.

2. Use command aliases.

If you always run a command with the same set of options, you can have bash create an alias for it. This alias will incorporate the required options, so that you don't need to remember them or manually type them every time. For example, if you always run `ls` with the `-l` option to obtain a detailed directory listing, you can use this command:

```
bash> alias ls='ls -l'
```

To create an alias that automatically includes the -l option. Once this alias has been created, typing *ls* at the bash prompt will invoke the alias and produce the `ls -l` output.

You can obtain a list of available aliases by invoking `alias` without any arguments, and you can delete an alias with `unalias`.

3. Use filename auto-completion.

Bash supports filename auto-completion at the command prompt. To use this feature, type the first few letters of the file name, followed by [Tab]. Bash will scan the current directory, as well as all other directories in the search path, for matches to that name. If a single match is found, bash will automatically complete the file name for you. If multiple matches are found, you will be prompted to choose one.

4. Use key shortcuts to efficiently edit the command-line.

Bash supports a number of keyboard shortcuts for command-line navigation and editing. The Ctrl-A key shortcut moves the cursor to the beginning of the command line, while the `Ctrl-E` shortcut moves the cursor to the end of the command line. The `Ctrl-W` shortcut deletes the word immediately before the cursor, while the `Ctrl-K` shortcut deletes everything immediately after the cursor. You can undo a deletion with `Ctrl-Y`.

5. Get automatic notification of new mail.

You can configure bash to automatically notify you of new mail, by setting the `$MAILPATH` variable to point to your local mail spool. For example, the command:

```
bash> MAILPATH='/var/spool/mail/john'

bash> export MAILPATH
```

Causes bash to print a notification on john's console every time a new message is appended to john's mail spool.

6. Run tasks in the background.

Bash lets you run one or more tasks in the background and selectively suspend or resume any of the current tasks (or "jobs"). To run a task in the background, add an ampersand (&) to the end of its command line. Here's an example:

```
bash> tail -f /var/log/messages &

[1] 614
```

Each task backgrounded in this manner is assigned a job ID, which is printed to the console. A task can be brought back to the foreground with the command `fg jobnumber`, where *`jobnumber`* is the job ID of the task you wish to bring to the foreground. Here's an example:

```
bash> fg 1
```

A list of active jobs can be obtained at any time by typing *jobs* at the bash prompt.

7. Quickly jump to frequently-used directories.

You probably already know that the `$PATH` variable lists bash's "search path"—the directories it will search when it can't find the requested file in the current directory. However, bash also supports the `$CDPATH` variable, which lists the directories the cd command will look in when attempting to change directories. To use this feature, assign a directory list to the `$CDPATH` variable, as shown in the example below:

```
bash> CDPATH='.:~:/usr/local/apache/htdocs:/disk1/backups'

bash> export CDPATH
```

Now, whenever you use the cd command, bash will check all the directories in the `$CDPATH` list for matches to the directory name.

8. Perform calculations.

Bash can perform simple arithmetic operations at the command prompt. To use this feature, simply type in the arithmetic expression you wish to evaluate at the prompt within double parentheses, as illustrated below. Bash will attempt to perform the calculation and return the answer.

```
bash> echo $((16/2))

8
```

9. Customize the shell prompt.

You can customize the bash shell prompt to display—among other things—the current user name and host name, the current time, the load average, and/or the current working directory. To do this, alter the `$PS1` variable, as below:

```
bash> PS1='\u@\h:\w \@> '

bash> export PS1

root@medusa:/tmp 03:01 PM>
```

This will display the name of the currently logged-in user, the host name, the current working directory, and the current time at the shell prompt. You can obtain a list of symbols understood by bash from its manual page.

10. Get context-specific help.

Bash comes with help for all built-in commands. To see a list of all built-in commands, type *help*. To obtain help on a specific command, type *help command*, where *command* is the command you need help on. Here's an example:

```
bash> help alias

...some help text...
```

Obviously, you can obtain detailed help on the bash shell by typing man bash at your command prompt at any time. ❖

Notes:

Hardware

10 ways to get your help desk ready to support a new rollout

By Mitch Bryant

Successfully rolling out a new application or system does not end when the "switch" is flipped on for all users. More often than not, the help desk must still cope with the users' need for support as the project rollout finishes. These tips will help your staff ramp up to deliver the necessary level of support with the least amount of chaos.

1. Get involved (way) early.

The help desk (and its support needs) always seem to be the last item on the checklist for most projects. This means the expertise of the help desk staff isn't being used as the project unfolds. Most project managers, support analysts, and vendors concentrate on the high-level issues. Then, typically, near the end of the project, they tend to provide limited support information to the help desk, almost as an afterthought.

To counter this tendency, the help desk must have sufficient involvement early enough in the project to get ready to address the questions and needs the users will have as the project gets rolled out to them. One of the best ways to ensure this involvement is to use a form to gather pertinent information that can be shared among support staff. The "Program rollout preparation checklist," available at http://techrepublic.com.com/5138-10877-6042399.html, is an excellent tool for nailing down the details that the help desk will need on a project, such as program, login, and printing requirements; affected users; security information; support options; and documentation.

2. Train the users... then train the help desk.

As projects are rolled out, user manuals are created and instructor-led or CBT classes are used to train end users, but what about the help desk support team? Consider sending some or all team members to the end users' training. If full training isn't feasible or necessary, you can create a condensed version. Even some familiarity with the processes will help your staff understand and resolve the problems users encounter.

3. Get screen shots of install and setup.

Nothing is worse than having to walk users through a procedure or task without the benefit of seeing the menus or options. Have a small set of team members install the application and make notes of potential issues and document them.

Remember: The support team will be asked setup questions, so they need to be familiar with this process. If the help desk is supporting multiple versions of an application, get a step-by-step screen shot of each version.

4. Prepare to support remote users as well as internal users.

Document unique or special support needs that differ between internal use and external remote use of an application/device. Not only will the support be different, but more often than not, the support team can't simply remote in and "take care of the issue."

5. Create an installation package.

Use a software installation package tool to create a consolidated package. This will save time, reduce inconsistencies, and take the guesswork out of the application installation process.

6. Assemble support documentation (with pictures).

Callers to the help desk are likely to need assistance with every aspect of the application. Put together documentation that includes instructions and images of login screens, install menus, special application screens, and setup screens.

7. Implement hotlines for immediate issues.

Depending on the size of the rollout and its impact on the organization, you may want to create a temporary hotline for users. This makes it easy for them to contact support staff who are trained to deal with immediate issues. You might also create a backdoor number that the support staff can use to quickly contact a senior support analyst for information or clarification during the first few days of a rollout.

8. Identify subject matter experts/senior end users.

Train one or more senior support staff members to serve as specialists for the application. You may also want to tap some of your more experienced end users to help other team members as needed. In fact, you might have a senior end user available at the help desk during the first few days of a major rollout. The advantage is that urgent how-to's are answered right away, and the senior end user gets a feel for what is going right and what is going wrong.

9. Create triage.

It's very important to the initial rollout and the ongoing support process that sound triage be developed by meeting with the vendor, support analyst, and members of the help desk. Make sure you've addressed these questions:

- What kind of issues can be expected?
- What common or known error messages will the help desk get calls about?

10. Prepare to address how-to concerns.

When a new application or device is rolled out, the help desk team is faced with fielding the everyday "how to" questions they get from end users. Although the team cannot be a subject matter expert in all aspects of the support model, they can assist with the most common five or 10 issues.

One good way to deal with ongoing support needs is to create a "top issues" cheat sheet for help desk staffers. This will allow even the less experienced help desk staff to identify and resolve a high percentage of problems. ❖

10+ things you should know about troubleshooting a slow PC

By Debra Shinder and Greg Shultz

User complaints are minimal when new PCs are rolled out. They start up quickly, and programs seem to open in a snap. But over time, the user begins to notice that the system is slow or that it hangs up often. While the possible causes for system slowdown are endless, I have identified 10 common troubleshooting areas you should examine first before you suggest to management that it's time for an upgrade.

1. Spyware and viruses

Spyware and viruses pose a significant security threat, and they can also dramatically decrease computer performance. The first step when combating spyware should always be to scan the machine with updated spyware detection/removal and antivirus software. Use these applications to remove any detected infections. If the software scanners don't work, here are a few other steps to try.

To remove spyware:

- Identify and end suspicious processes with Windows Task Manager.
- Identify and disable suspicious services with the Management Console.
- Identify and disable suspicious services and startup items with the System Configuration Utility.
- Search and delete registry entries associated with suspicious services or startup items.
- Identify and delete suspicious files.
- Install and use multiple spyware detection and removal utilities.

Note: If the above techniques fail, start Windows in Safe Mode and retry.

Virus removal techniques depend heavily on the specific virus variant. You must therefore tailor your removal efforts to each virus. Here is a list of TechRepublic resources for removing common viruses and worms:

- Identify/React Chart: Sober.P (http://techrepublic.com.com/5138-1009-5693436.html)
- Identify/React Chart: Cabir (http://techrepublic.com.com/5138-1035-5519369.html)
- Identify/React Chart: Mugly (http://techrepublic.com.com/5138-1035-5489218.html)
- Identify/React Chart: Atak (http://techrepublic.com.com/5138-1035-5489194.html)

- Identify/React Chart: Maslan (http://techrepublic.com.com/5138-1035-5489190.html)
- Identify/React Chart: Anzae/Inzae (http://techrepublic.com.com/5138-1035-5489168.html)
- Identify/React Chart: Zafi (http://techrepublic.com.com/5138-1035-5489124.html)
- Identify/React Chart: Netsky (http://techrepublic.com.com/5138-1035-5488932.html)
- Identify/React Chart: Sober.I/Sober.J (http://techrepublic.com.com/5138-1035-5481090.html)
- Identify/React Chart: Bofra (http://techrepublic.com.com/5138-1035-5475155.html)
- Identify/React Chart: Bagle.AZ (Beagle.AR Symantec) (http://techrepublic.com.com/5138-1035-5392108.html)
- Identify/React Chart: Korgo.A (aka Bloodhound or Padobot) and variants (http://techrepublic.com.com/5138-1035-5323818.html)
- Identify/React Chart: Lovegate (http://techrepublic.com.com/5138-1035-5315085.html)
- Identify/React Chart: MyDoom (http://techrepublic.com.com/5138-1035-5316934.html)
- Identify/React chart: Bagle virus (http://techrepublic.com.com/5138-1035-5290719.html)

2. Processor overheating

Modern processors generate a lot of heat. That's why all processors require some sort of cooling element, typically a fan of some type. Machines used for gaming or other processor-intensive activities often use more sophisticated water cooling or refrigerant systems. When the processor temperature goes over spec, the system can slow down or run erratically. Modern motherboards can monitor the processor temperature and report it through the system BIOS.

The processor fan may fail for several reasons:

- Dust is preventing the fan from spinning smoothly.
- The fan motor has failed.
- The fan bearings are loose and "jiggling."

Often you can tell if there is a fan problem by listening and/or touching the computer. A fan that has loose bearings starts jiggling and vibrates the case, making a characteristic noise. You may barely notice the noise at first, and it's common for even the experienced computer pro to overlook this change. But as time goes by, the sounds and vibrations will become so prominent that you'll change the fan out just to stop the racket!

You don't always need to replace the fan. If it is covered with dust, you can often spray away the dust with compressed air. Note that even though you might get the fan running again, its life span has likely been reduced because of the overwork. You should keep an extra fan in reserve in case of failure.

There are a number of software utilities that will track the temperature of your processor and case. If you want to try some of these utilities, check out CNET's Download.com at http://www.download.com/ and use the search term "temperature."

3. Bad RAM

Several situations can lead to a bad RAM relationship with a particular machine:

- RAM timing is slower than optimal machine spec.
- RAM has minor flaws that only appear on detailed testing.
- RAM is overheating.

In the "old days" of Fast Page RAM, buying new RAM for your computer was a pretty simple affair. You just needed to know what speed your motherboard supported and the maximum each slot would take. Today, there are many different speeds and types of RAM, and the better motherboards may be tolerant of using RAM that does not match the motherboard's maximum specs. For example, your motherboard may support ECC RAM but will still work with non-ECC RAM, or may support both PC2700 and PC3200 DIMMs. But be aware that you may need to change BIOS settings and you may see performance decreases if you install RAM that is slower than the maximum spec.

Minor flaws in RAM chips can lead to system slowdowns and instability. The least expensive chips often have minor flaws that will cause your system to slow down or Blue Screen intermittently. Although built-in mechanisms may allow the system to keep working, there is a performance hit when it has to deal with flawed RAM chips.

In the past, no one worried about RAM chips getting hot, because they didn't seem to generate much heat. But that's changed with newer RAM types, especially SDRAM. To check for overheating, open your computer's case, power down, and pull the plug out. Ground yourself and touch the plastic on one of your RAM chips. Ouch! They get pretty hot. If you find that your RAM chips are overheating, you should consider buying a separate fan to cool your memory. If your motherboard doesn't support a RAM fan, you might be able to get enough additional cooling by installing a fan card that plugs into a PCI slot.

You can also buy copper "heatspreaders" or RAM heatsinks that improve heat dissipation and help prevent problems caused by overheated RAM.

Tip: Some motherboards will even allow you to mix speeds but will default to the slowest RAM installed.

4. Failing hard disk

There may be many signs of imminent failure before a hard disk finally gives up, depending on the type of failure (mechanical, electronic, logical, or firmware failure). Some of these signs include:

- Slow access times on the affected drive
- An increasing number of bad sectors when running scandisk and chkdsk
- Unexplained Blue Screens
- Intermittent boot failures

Detecting a failing hard disk can be tricky because the early signs are subtle. Experienced computer professionals can often hear a change in the normal disk spin (often manifested as a clicking or crunching noise or a high-pitched whine). After the disk deteriorates further, you'll see the system crawl to a standstill. Write processes will take a long time as the system tries to find good blocks to write to. (This will occur if you're using a robust file system such as NTFS; other file systems will likely Blue Screen the computer.) You may get error messages such as *Windows delayed write failure* on Windows computers.

When you notice the system slow down, run scandisk or chkdsk, depending on your operating system. If you notice a bad sector where a good sector existed earlier, that's a clue that the disk is going bad. Back up the data on the disk and prepare for it to fail soon. Make sure you have a spare disk ready so you can replace it when it fails, or replace the disk as soon as you notice the early signs of failure.

Disk noise and scandisk/chkdsk are your best indicators for identifying a failing drive that's leading to a system slowdown. However, if you are managing a system remotely, or you can't take the system down for a full chkdsk/R, you can use tools that monitor disk health, such as Executive Software's DiskAlert (http://www.execsoft.com/diskalert/diskalert.asp).

5. BIOS settings

One often-ignored culprit of system slowdown is the machine's BIOS settings. Most people accept the BIOS settings as they were configured in the factory and leave them as is. However, slowdowns may occur if the BIOS settings do not match the optimal machine configuration. Often you can improve machine performance by researching your motherboard's optimal BIOS settings—which may not be the same as the factory defaults.

There is no centralized database of optimal BIOS settings, but a simple Web search on your motherboard name and BIOS as keywords should yield the correct settings.

You may also be able to increase performance by updating or "flashing" your BIOS. Check with your motherboard's vendor for the software and instructions to do this.

6. Disk type/controller compatibility

You've just purchased a new UDMA-100 disk drive, and it doesn't seem any faster than any of the other drives in your machine. You do some benchmark testing, and the new disk tests the same as the other drives in your system. So what's the problem?

It could be that your motherboard doesn't support the UDMA 100 specification. Check your manual to determine what type of IDE interface it supports. If the motherboard only supports UDMA 33 or 66, then your UDMA 100 throttles down for backwards compatibility. You can get around this problem by installing a PCI UDMA 100 add-on card and plugging the new drive in to that interface.

Another potential problem may be the cable type you are using. UDMA 66+ drives require a different cable than older drive types. The drive may not work at all with the old cable type. Aged cables will break down over time, especially if they are tightly folded and the temperature of the case remains consistently high. It's always worthwhile to change out the drive cable to see if performance improves.

Also keep in mind that over the course of a year to 18 months, hard disk technology improves so that performance of newer disks is substantially greater (and so are disk capacities). Replacing older disks, even if they are not at risk of failure, can give you a big performance boost. New Serial ATA (SATA) disks are faster than old Parallel ATA types.

7. Windows services

Many Windows services are enabled by default. Many of these services, however, are not required for your machine to run properly. You should review the services running on your Windows 2000/Windows XP computer and disable those that you don't need.

One way to see what services are running is to use the Services applet found in the Administrative Tools menu. Right-click My Computer and select Manage. Important information contained in the Services console includes the service Name, Status, and Startup Type. You can get more details on a service by double-clicking on it to bring up the service's Properties.

You can stop the service by clicking the Stop button. If you are sure that you don't need the service, click the down arrow in the Startup Type drop-down list box and set the service to Disabled. If you are not sure if you need the service, change the Startup Type to Manual. Then you'll have the option of manually starting the service if you find that you need it.

Another way of controlling which services start is using the msconfig utility. Open the Run dialog box and type *msconfig* in the Open text box. The Essential column shows services Microsoft considers essential to running the computer. However, note that many required services are not defined as essential in the System

Configuration Utility window. You can prevent a service from starting at bootup by unchecking the check box to the left of the service.

One service that is well known for slowing down Windows 2000/Windows XP systems is the Indexing Service. This service indexes the content of each hard disk and makes it easier for the Search utility to find files. Unless you are running a Web site that uses the indexing service, you may want to disable it to improve performance.

8. Runaway processes

Runaway processes take up all of the processors' cycles. The usual suspects are badly written device drivers and legacy software installed on a newer operating system. You can identify a runaway process by looking at the process list in the Windows Task Manager. Any process that takes almost 100 percent of the processing time is likely a runaway process.

There are exceptions to this rule. On a smoothly running system, the System Idle Process should be consuming the majority of the processor cycles most of the time. If any other process were to take up 98 percent of the processor cycles, you might have a runaway process.

If you do find a runaway process, you can right-click the process and click the End Process command. You may need to stop some processes, such as runaway system services, from the Services console. If you can't stop the service using the console, you may need to reboot the system. Sometimes a hard reboot is required.

9. Disk fragmentation

As files are added, deleted, and changed on a disk, the contents of the file can become spread across sectors located in disparate regions of the disk. This is file fragmentation. Some older operating systems, such as Windows NT, don't have a built-in defrag utility; you must obtain a third-party solution, such as Executive Software's Diskeeper (http://www.execsoft.com/diskeeper/diskeeper.asp).

Disk fragmentation can significantly slow down your machine. The disk heads must move back and forth while seeking all the fragments of a file. A common cause of disk fragmentation is a disk that is too full. You should keep 20 percent to 25 percent of your hard disk space free to minimize file fragmentation and to improve the defragmenter's ability to defrag the disk. Thus, if a disk is too full, move some files off the drive and restart the defragmenter.

In Windows XP, you can use the defrag.exe command-line tool to schedule defragmentation on a regular basis. For Windows 2000, you can use a program such as AutoDefrag (see http://techrepublic.com.com/5100-1035-1048744.html) to schedule defragmentation.

10. Background applications

Have you ever visited an end-user's desktop and noticed a dozen icons in the system tray? Each icon represents a process running in either the foreground or background. Most of them are running in the background, so the users may not be aware that they are running 20+ applications at the same time.

This is due to applications starting up automatically in the background. Look first for such programs in the Startup folder in the Start menu. Many applications place components in the Startup folder to run in the background. Some of these, such as the Microsoft Office Findfast, can really chew up processor and disk time and noticeably slow down a system. Review each of the entries in the Startup folder and delete any that are unnecessary.

Not all programs that run at startup appear in the Startup folder. Another place to look is the following registry keys: HKEY_ LOCAL_MACHINE\Software\Microsoft\Windows\CurrentVersion\Run and HKEY_LOCAL_MACHINE\Software\Microsoft\Windows\CurrentVersion\RunOnce.

In Windows XP, run `msconfig` and check the Startup tab to view startup programs. You can uncheck the boxes to keep individual programs from running at startup.

11. File system issues

Some file systems work better than others for large disk partitions. If the machine runs Windows NT 4.0, Windows 2000, or Windows XP, you should use the NTFS file system for best performance.

File system performance is closely related to cluster size and the number of clusters on the disk. NTFS file systems will bog down if you have a 60-GB hard disk configured with a cluster size of 512 bytes. This creates an enormous number of clusters, which the file system must track and seek. This becomes especially problematic when the drive is highly fragmented. One solution is to use larger cluster sizes. If you set the cluster size to 4K or larger, you will see noticeable improvement in file load times. Please note, however, that large clusters can significantly increase the amount of cluster slack space and lead to a lot of wasted disk space.

Another trick to alleviate file system issues involves tweaking some Registry values (Start Menu | Run | Regedit):

- The first Registry value you can tweak is NtfsDisable8dot3NameCreation, which can be found at HKEY_LOCAL_MACHINE\SYSTEM\Current ControlSet\Control\Filesystem. When you set this value to 1, it stops NTFS from generating the 8.3 file-naming convention used for backward compatibility. If you do not need these old filenames, you can improve performance by preventing NTFS from creating them.

- Another useful NTFS entry is the NtfsDisableLastAccess value, which can be found at HKEY_LOCAL_MACHINE\SYSTEM\CurrentControlSet\Control\Filesystem. This is a REG_DWORD entry, and when it is set to 1, it will prevent NTFS from updating the date and time stamp of directories after they are browsed. However, this does not prevent an update to the file-access information when a file is opened or changed.

If you are not using the NTFS file system, you may be able to improve performance by moving files and folders out of the root directory. With FAT partitions, you may notice a big slowdown in system performance after running scandisk because a large number of .chk files are placed in the root directory. Users sometimes fill their root directories by making it the default file storage location. Move as many files and folders as possible out of the root directory, and performance should improve significantly. ❖

10 things you should know about deploying technology in harsh environments

By Rick Vanover

If you've ever had to put a computer in a shop environment, you know that its lifecycle may be shortened—even halved—by exposure to high temperatures, moisture, air particulate, or other irritants to electronics. Here are some lessons learned from deploying technology in harsh environments that will help you maintain the IT equipment lifecycle in the worst of conditions.

1. Solutions for visibility and security

As many members will attest, having good visibility is key to being able to support a critical piece of equipment that's outside the data center—and possibly at a location that has no IT staff. This goes for harsh environments as well. Products today offer many solutions to ensure both visibility and security so that operators (and anyone else) can see "the red light" on the server or whatever is deployed.

From outside the enclosure, you can:

- See which server is powered on (with this equipment, green is on, amber is off).
- See which hard drives are spinning (green is running, black is off, red is failed).
- See the blue UID (unit identifier) light on the server (a handy feature of ProLiant servers).
- Determine whether the external hard drive array (top) is spinning all drives.

This enclosure has a lockable front panel to keep unwanted users out. Note that the batteries are outside the enclosure. In this case, this was done to reduce the exhaust inside the enclosure.

If you choose this option, bear in mind that you may or may not be able to fully support the system entirely remotely.

2. Selecting an enclosure and air conditioner

This market has many offerings covering a range of quality, features, and price. When deciding on an enclosure, make sure you can accurately calculate:

- Interior dimensions
- Weight capacity and overall weight
- Ergonomic considerations
- Cable entry/exit accessibility

Most enclosures allow you obtain detailed technical information. ITS Enclosures offers good technical information for your planning phase.

You may need to deploy an air conditioner with the enclosure, and most providers will help you select the correctly powered air conditioner for the system you're implementing, sell you the unit, and attach it to the enclosure. Be sure not to underprovision a system in cooling management from the start. Thermal overloads in your integrated management logs are not pleasant.

Most, if not all, enclosure air conditioners detail their information on the exterior in a visible manner.

This label indicates that the air conditioner can operate between 3800 and 4000 BTU for thermal cooling. The power requirements and thermal ranges are also detailed.

A good rule of thumb is to add approximately 35-percent utilization to your base BTU requirement to ensure adequate thermal provisioning. Also consider using TFT screens instead of CRT monitors for less thermal strain on the interior.

3. Power provisioning

Although most IT staffers are familiar with getting basic power service in the data center, getting selected power in other locations brings new challenges. When working with non-data center locations, be sure that you clearly communicate the power requirements with the following traits:

- Provide quantity and connection type requirements (e.g., QTY 2 NEMA L5-30P would be the "30 Amp Twist Lock" that is used by many UPS units).
- Provide a picture of the connection type—you can obtain this from the technical information of all products you're feeding.
- Request separate circuits for your power protection (UPS) and air conditioner unit.
- Know the input voltage requirements.

4. Drainage for thermal management

This may be a peculiar topic, but many air conditioners rely on standard evaporation from a small tray for the liquid discharge that it pulls from the interior air. As the air becomes more conditioned, less humidity will come from the interior, but there's still a drainage factor. Drainage can't be ignored, especially if there's frequent access to the inside of the enclosure.

Two basic options are available:

- A heated metal plate that causes instant evaporation of the drip condensations
- A bucket and flex tubing

The bucket and flex tubing may sound unsophisticated, but it's a $10 solution that's quite manageable, and it doesn't take much effort to install. The heated plates require additional power, and installation is not at all pleasant.

5. Planning for accessibility

Just like in the data room, where you can extend a server out of a rack, you should be able to do the same from the enclosure in the remote environment. Many full specification rack enclosures allow you to mount standard servers and fully extend forward. This makes installation and serviceability much easier. You can also likely utilize cable management arms in these types of enclosures.

6. Ensuring phone line proximity

All IT staffers surely have access to a mobile phone, but it's still a good idea to have a telephone line close to the remote enclosure. Support is much easier for operational staff (who may not have mobile phones), as well as vendors who may be collaborating on the remote technology in the enclosure. Regardless of the user, having a phone line accessible, or even in the cabinet, can greatly reduce the time to identify and communicate a potential issue, as well as increasing possible operational benefits. A phone line also has a possible use as a contingency modem if the network link to this station fails.

7. Dealing with extreme cold

This may sound like a thermal management nonissue, right? Think again. Having deployed technology solutions in freezer areas of food distribution centers, I've learned that you may not be able to rely on the exhaust of a system to provide adequate heat. For example, most technology equipment's operating temperature range is 50 degrees F on the bottom end. This is a far cry from the -40 degree F environments in a large freezer complex. While operating, a device may make enough exhaust heat to keep it in the operating range. However during storage or idle times, you run the risk of damaging the components and possibly voiding the warranty, as ice may form on the inside of the components.

Just as air conditioners can keep enclosures cool, thermal management heating solutions can keep an enclosure in an operating range for equipment. Be sure to get one with thermostat-like control because if the ambient temperature gets within a tolerable range, you want the heating source to idle so it won't overheat the interior. This is especially important if you deploy a solution that uses a cold, or idle, secondary system.

8. Facilitating support by nontechnical staff

Visibility and labeling are important for technology deployed in harsh environments. You may not have IT staff working with the system, and certain operational and troubleshooting elements may be done by facility maintenance staff, operational staff, managers, or other non-IT individuals.

For example, take a rackthat a TechRepublic member recently implemented for a customer solution. The rack uses intuitive connectivity and labeling as follows:

- Red cables are Ethernet networking cables going to a local switch.
- Gray cables are special long-haul serial lines going to an Ethernet-attached multiport serial adapter.
- Each cable end is labeled for its role.
- A label panel on the cable management identifies each network port.
- Cable management flex conduit keeps like cables together and runs snug through the enclosure.

9. Preventive maintenance on the air conditioner

If your enclosure has an air conditioner with a replaceable air filter, be sure to replace it. These are not expensive pieces but are critical to the effective operation of the air conditioner in filtering airborne particulate from entering the controlled environment inside the enclosure.

The other important preventative maintenance task is to ensure that the air conditioner has adequate Freon. A common strategy is to make a facility maintenance staff responsible for replacing the air filters and keeping the Freon charged.

10. Consolidated technology spots

Many factories, shops, and distribution centers have networking cabinets/enclosures on the floor to extend the network infrastructure for the technology elements. These enclosures are generally not in environmentally controlled enclosures. If you deploy larger systems (e.g., servers or critical workstations) in a harsh environment and have a full-size enclosure, consider consolidating the network infrastructure into the same enclosure for a smaller IT footprint and consolidated enclosure space. ❖

10 things you should know about building a PC from scratch

By Erik Eckel

With an ever-expanding array of barebones kit options, a growing number of PC parts suppliers, and seven new versions of Microsoft's next Windows client coming, many technology professionals may choose to build custom systems from scratch. Doing so offers several advantages, including the ability to tailor components to your needs while controlling costs. This list offers 10 recommendations to review when building a PC from the ground up.

1. Select the mobo carefully.

The motherboard is the most important component you select when building a PC from scratch. Not only does your motherboard choice determine the number and type of ports (parallel, serial, USB, memory card, etc.) a new system possesses, but it also dictates which processor powers the box, the memory (type and speed) that's used, the number and type of disks (IDE, SATA, etc.) supported, and the resulting PC case style (micro, Shuttle, mid-tower, 1U server, etc.), as the motherboard's form factor (ATX, mini-ITX, etc.) typically determines the case that must be used.

Pay particular attention to a motherboard's CPU socket type when reviewing your processor options. The CPU socket type typically dictates the CPU manufacturer (Intel versus AMD) as well as the processor family (Pentium 4, Athlon, Celeron, Sempron, etc.). If you become confused as to which socket is designed for which CPU, Wikipedia maintains a handy listing (http://en.wikipedia.org/wiki/List_of_CPU_sockets).

It's also a good idea to review the motherboard's chipset and video port specifications. Chipset type determines maximum RAM configuration (among other elements), while most every contemporary board supports older PCI technology. Newer boards, however, favor PCI-Express slots over AGP for improved video performance.

2. Review CPU options.

While your motherboard choice often determines the processor (AMD Athlon 64-bit and Intel Core Duo are but two examples), you still have a decision to make. That is, how fast should your processor be?

Remember that a CPU boasting additional processor cycles will provide improved performance during its service life, and the service life may well be extended proportionate to its increase in speed over base models. In other words, a Pentium 4 3.06 GHz chip is more likely to meet minimum system requirements longer than the same model CPU with a 2.26 GHz clock.

3. Don't skimp on the PC case.

Avoid the temptation to purchase the cheapest beige box. The case that houses the system does more than just hold the PC's components. Cases also determine the system's footprint, as well as the type and number of data ports easily accessed from the machine's front.

4. Power up.

Never underestimate the importance of a good power supply. Problematic power supplies can be a nightmare to diagnose. Ensure that you purchase a quality unit that generates sufficient power for your system's configuration.

5. Check the RAM.

You can never have enough RAM, but you can certainly purchase it improperly. For example, if you need 2 GB of RAM, don't plan on plugging four 512 MB sticks into most boards. Many motherboards now feature only a pair of RAM slots, so be sure to purchase the most concentrated RAM modules you can.

Also, purchase the correct memory. It's easy to confuse different types. Confirm that you've received the proper RAM and aren't the recipient of 333 MHz DDR memory when you paid for a 400 MHz DDR stick, as almost happened to me recently. (Fortunately, I caught the error and corrected a well-intentioned clerk prior to completing the purchase.)

6. Choose the right disk format.

Your motherboard selection will provide you with several disk options. In addition to the requisite CD/DVD drive, you'll likely have your choice of IDE, SATA, or even SCSI hard disks. If your system will process large amounts of data often, it's worth supplying the new system with a SATA or SCSI drive.

But if the system is to be used for nonintensive applications (likely the case for the majority of corporate systems), cheaper and potentially recyclable IDE hard disks are readily available and will adequately meet your needs. Don't just assume you need the latest and greatest hardware. Significant savings can be had by reusing an existing 5400 RPM 20 GB IDE disk as opposed to purchasing a new 7,200 RPM 300 GB SATA drive.

7. Consider video requirements.

There used to be little call for potent video cards in most corporate environments. Other than graphic artists, CAD designers, professional photographers, and video production houses, few people other than gamers really required video cards packing more than even 64 MB of video RAM.

But that's all changing. The use of rich media is growing exponentially across all professions. The trend is sure to stress a vast number of video cards currently in use, and Windows Vista (with its graphically intensive Glass interface) will push many organizations to using video cards with 256 MB or more RAM.

Video adapter type is another consideration when building a barebones system. PCI- and AGP-based adapters long met most organization's needs. But PCI-Express, with higher speeds resulting from serial interconnects versus the old-style bus, is overtaking AGP (which itself overtook PCI).

Be sure to keep your organization's requirements, and the system's intended use, in mind when specifying the new PC's video parameters. In many cases, a simple embedded video adapter will meet your needs. In others, a separate AGP or PCI-E slot and video adapter with 256 MB nonshared video RAM may be required to accommodate graphically intensive tasks.

8. Secure everything.

More than a few systems have been hastily built and pressed into service. It's easy to overlook fundamentals, especially when projects stack up, but always take the extra time to secure all the components inside a PC.

Ensure all power supply and data cables are directed away from cooling fans, including fans used to cool the CPU, video card, and the case itself. PCs have lots of moving parts, so prevent cables from shifting position by connecting them to the case's frame (or even other cables) using zip ties.

Also take time to secure all drives and disks in their bays. Don't rely upon a single screw to hold a hard disk or CD/DVD drive in place; use at least two screws (one to each side) and preferably four (two to a side).

9. Buy a burner.

If 40 is the new 30, a CD/DVD burner is the new floppy. Many PCs no longer even include a floppy disk. Assuming a little extra cost now (for a CD or DVD writing drive) will save you time and trouble in the future.

Sure, everyone believes they'll be able to e-mail or FTP larger files to the appropriate vendor, supplier, or customer, but I've lost count of the number of times I've needed to transfer large files but couldn't access FTP shares due to security or firewall issues and couldn't e-mail the files due to Exchange attachment restrictions.

Add a burner to your barebones PC and you'll also have a secondary method of creating backups, too. The benefits simply outweigh the costs.

10. Cool is good; heat is bad.

PC cases commonly don't include five-dollar case fans. Buy one and install it. Heat's a PC's worst enemy.

Purchase a quality CPU fan, too. Both cheap and expensive models (particularly any that add neon glow) should be avoided. Instead, go with tried-and-true manufacturers that don't make CPU cooling complicated. It's a simple problem with a simple solution.

Also, don't store the system's documentation inside the PC. I recently replaced a failed hard disk in a physician's computer that likely died an early death because the previous administrator placed a plastic bag containing the PC's documentation inside the case. It's a practice I see occasionally. Although it's a good idea in concept (keeping a system's documentation, license, and install CD with the unit), the material obstructs airflow. In this case, it blocked numerous exhaust ports and likely contributed to the hard drive's premature failure. ❖

10 things you can do to optimize and maintain your PCs

Compiled by TechRepublic Staff

Everyone knows that the key to keeping equipment in peak condition—whether it's a chain saw, a motorcycle, or a desktop PC—is to follow a preemptive maintenance routine. The question is, what sort of maintenance tasks are required? In a shop full of hundreds (or thousands) of PCs, a systematic approach is essential. This list offers 10 basic measures to incorporate into your optimization and maintenance routine.

1. Regularly run Defrag and the Disk Cleanup Tool on client systems.

Disk fragmentation, especially on intensively used systems, will degrade performance over time. Just be careful about running disk defragmentation when large files are open. For example, if a transactional database (SQL or MSDE) is running, defragmentation tools can't exclusively access all or parts of these types of files to defrag the disk. If there is a service that you can stop to bring this part of the system to a zero-transaction state, you will be able to defrag the drive much more effectively. This is a good task to automate by using a third-party tool like DisKeeper (http://www.diskeeper.com/defrag.asp).

Running Disk Cleanup can optimize systems by emptying the Recycle Bin, Temporary Setup Files, Downloaded Program Files, Temporary Internet Files, Old Chkdsk Files, Temporary Files, Temporary Offline Files, Offline Files, etc. To ensure regular execution, you can run the tool as a scheduled task.

2. Keep firmware and drivers up to date.

Firmware updates can keep systems and subsystems current for the best performance. (Be sure to test the functionality before deploying firmware updates and keep a revision of the firmware distributions you're using or have previously used; you may need that archived version again.)

Driver updates can also optimize performance. Keep a revision of the driver versions you use/have used. As with firmware, you may need an archived version in the future. (See "10 things you should know about device driver rollback in Windows XP" for some helpful pointers.)

3. Keep Windows and essential applications up to date.

Use Windows Update to pull down the updates (cautiously) or use Windows Server Update Services (http://www.microsoft.com/windowsserversystem/updateservices/

evaluation/default.mspx) to retrieve your approved list. Be aware of potential conflicts with service packs and updates. If PCs have other critical applications running (IIS, SQL, MSDE, etc.), apply the appropriate service packs as they become available. For Microsoft applications, check the Baseline Security Analyzer (http://www.microsoft.com/technet/security/tools/mbsahome.mspx) to determine service pack levels.

4. Keep antivirus and anti-spyware definitions up to date.

Consider using automatic updates to pull down the latest definitions for your programs. Use tools like Ad-Aware (http://www.lavasoftusa.com/software/adaware/) by Lavasoft for extra protection against Trojans, browser hijacking, and other malicious activities.

5. Inspect Services configuration and Device Manager.

Open the Services applet of the Windows Control Panel to verify that the Windows-based services that are running and set to Automatic at startup are consistent with your configuration. (For more on enabling/disabling services, see "Windows XP services that can be disabled" (http://techrepublic.com.com/5138-10877-5747817.html) and "Video: Disable and enable Windows XP services" (http://techrepublic.com.com/5138-10877-6040912.html).)

Open the Windows Device Manager to look for any devices that are not operating correctly or that may have been removed. Subsystem components may report an error if they're incorrectly configured or not working.

6. Check page file configuration.

Open virtual memory configuration and make sure that the page file size and location are correct for the amount of free space on the drive and the amount of memory installed on the system.

7. Check power quality.

If you have a UPS battery, ensure that it is satisfied with the power supplied to it. If you aren't using one, check that the power source is a good circuit and is correctly grounded. Also make sure that surge suppression strips are in use.

8. Stay on top of cleaning tasks.

Perform a periodic full system cleaning by taking the system apart, removing all dust, and cleaning the external and internal surfaces of the computer. (If you don't have a cleaning solution, you can make one for external surfaces out of 1:1 rubbing alcohol and water.) Be sure to unplug the electronic components when introducing a solution and allow it to dry fully. You should also:

- Clean the keyboard and mouse. Use a dust vacuum and the alcohol/water solution to clean these dust- and dirt-collecting components.
- Run a CD-ROM cleaner. As with audio systems, CD-ROM drives can be cleaned with special kits for disc cleaning.
- Clean display devices by using a cleaner to remove fingerprints, dust, and other imperfections on the screen.
- Hit floppy drives, if you have them, with a good blast of canned air to remove dust accumulations. Use covers/panels if available to help keep dust out of the drives.
- If your systems have tape drives, run a cleaning tape through to keep the tape heads clean.

9. Ensure proper operating area environment.

Monitor the area for acceptable temperatures (somewhere between 60 and 77 degrees Fahrenheit) and good air quality. Watch out for tobacco smoke, manufacturing environments, and paper dust. If conditions are less than favorable, you might consider an environmental enclosure.

Check inside and outside the computer for proper airflow. You don't want a computer being used inside a box or pushed into a corner, and you don't want to see a hard drive or other internal device incorrectly installed and blocking airflow to other components. While you're at it, check for all necessary screws on the case and make sure that the case lid or panels are fixed down on all sides. With some systems, case panels are critical to the internal airflow for components.

10. Check internal and external connections.

Open the system and verify that all connections feel solid and are placed correctly. Double-check any accessory cards for a snug setting and good connections.

Make sure cable tensions are appropriate. Having too much strain on a cable or connection can damage the cable, device, jack/node, or the computer. Be sure that there is plenty of slack in the cables on the device and computer ends. Excess strain may cause intermittent performance issues. ❖

10 things you should know before buying satellite broadband Internet service

By John McCormick

Until fairly recently if you were in a location without cable television service or further than a few miles from a telephone substation, you were stuck with dialup Internet service. The performance of high-speed wired services quickly degrade as you move further from the nearest telephone substation so, even if you can get a DSL line at the limits of availability, service is likely to be poor.

This has actually dictated the location of many businesses, requiring them to locate in more expensive areas. If you had a mobile service van or command center then the situation was even worse because you were stuck with a cellular link.

But today there are several one- and two-way satellite Internet providers with a variety of offerings for home users (for example, telecommuters or your company's key personnel), small businesses, even mobile labs, and field service units. This guide will focus mostly on two-way broadband but also offers a comparison with one-way broadband services. It provides a list of 10 critical issues you should consider before choosing satellite broadband and examines the advantages and disadvantages of one-way and two-way satellite systems.

1. You must have a secure and sufficient location to mount the disk.

You must own the property or have the rights to mount a 30-inch dish. The dish must be secure against vandalism and even casual contact because a two-way broadband service includes a powerful microwave transmitter, one capable of blasting a clear data signal to a geosynchronous satellite more than 20,000 miles away. The signal can cause serious burns if someone puts their hand or arm between the dish and the transmitter antenna. In addition to the question of landlord requirements, there may be zoning restrictions, although the dish is pretty small and relatively easy to conceal. The dish must also have an unobstructed view of the sky where the satellite is located.

2. You will experience latency.

The satellites are geosynchronous—fixed in position above the earth so satellite dishes can be pointed at the same location all the time. The orbits are about 22,390 miles above the equator because that makes their orbital period 23h 56m, the same as earth's rotation. The round-trip from your dish to the satellite is therefore about 47,000 miles which results in a speed-of-light delay amounting to almost a quarter of a second total, double that if the office at the other end is also on a satellite link. VoIP service may not be supported and telephone Internet calls may not be practical.

3. Upload speeds are limited.

There are very real limits to the upload bandwidth available with a small dish and, if it isn't enough for your needs then, you will have to consider a dedicated, hard-wired Internet connection. The inexpensive satellite broadband services are intended for small or branch offices with a workstation or two, perhaps a small network, not data centers.

4. Understand the pricing structure before purchase.

Ask the vendor for a breakdown of the services included with the monthly fee. Does that price include always-on service with unlimited broadband? Some services charge extra depending on the volume of traffic. Depending on whether you use a one-way or two-way system, you may be required to retain a dialup connection with separate ISP. You'll need to factor this into your monthly costs.

If you have multiple locations or a mix of mobile and fixed locations, does the vendor offer a discount for establishing multiple accounts? If the discount is small or nonexistent, consider using multiple vendors so maintenance outages would be spread out. There are some specialized vendors that can provide two-way broadband with mobile antennas.

5. The vendor may or may not guarantee a specific bandwidth level.

Ask the vendor if they provide a bandwidth guarantee. If they do offer a guarantee, make sure you fully understand the policy and know how to prove that the proper bandwidth is not provided. Most vendors publish a "fair use" policy that may limit your bandwidth during periods of peak usage. Others may require a service technician to perform bandwidth tests only with the vendor's Web site.

6. Make sure you will be notified during planned network outages.

Any complex system can suffer unexpected maintenance problems, but it's easier to cope with those if you are at least notified in advance of planned service outages. Find out if the vendor notify you of planned network outages and if so, how (telephone call, e-mail, etc.).

7. Your ability to easily upgrade service will depend on the installation and the vendor.

Increasing bandwidth may only require a quick call to the vendor and an increase in your monthly payment. You should avoid a service that would require new hardware or a visit from a technician, especially if you are starting with a low-bandwidth subscription as a test.

8. Own versus leased equiment.

Will you own or lease the hardware? Ask the vendor what a "standard" installation includes and cost. Satellite equipment can be expensive and, depending on how long you will use the equipment, leasing may make more sense. If you purchase the hardware, ensure you know the costs and provided warranty.

9. You may be locked in to a service contract.

Ensure you understand the vendor's minimum service contract. If the service doesn't meet your needs, can you cancel your purchase and return the equipment? Some providers won't let you cancel before the end of your initial contract even if the service doesn't meet your needs.

10. Understand the hardware/software requirements and network limitations.

Some systems require a dedicated server or at least a PC to be present at the terminal end. Others provide a high-speed modem that you can connect to any PC, router, or switch. If you need a static IP address, ensure the vendor can provide one. If you are considering voice over Internet protocol (VoIP), you should also ask if the vendor supports it.

Comparing different satellite broadband options

Satellite Internet services use geosynchronous satellites the same as the familiar television satellites and, with the exception of some rare weather conditions (mostly very heavy rain), provide fast, reliable Internet connections for up to about five concurrent users on a small network.

The most basic points to consider when narrowing the field of potential vendors are:

- One-way vs. two-way broadband satellite
- Minimum required speed
- Fixed vs. mobile location(s)

One-way vs. two-way systems

If you don't need fast uploads then a one-way satellite Internet system may be perfect. These use a standard dial-up account with a traditional modem to send requests or uploads to the Internet along with a receive-only dish to get the broadband inbound signal.

One-way satellite broadband

Advantages:

- Simple installation (you can do it yourself)
- Perhaps more economical service

Disadvantages:

- The need to maintain a dialup account
- The need for a dedicated phone line
- Increased latency because of the dual-path linkage
- Loss of services when phone lines are out of service

Two-way satellite broadband has signals going both ways to the satellite from your location. Upgrading your service is usually just a matter of calling customer service.

Two-way satellite broadband

Advantages

- Uploads are much faster than dialup even though they are slower than your download speeds
- No separate telephone line or dialup account is required, although you probably want a cheap dialup account available for emergencies.
- Your part of the installation can be as simple as connecting the vendor's modem to your network using standard 10/100 Ethernet cables—no special software or PC cards may be required.
- Always on service even if the phone network is out. This service will even operate during a local disaster such as the aftermath of a flood or a hurricane if you have a generator or large UPS.

Disadvantages:

- More expensive hardware
- Professional installation required—this isn't difficult but it involves sending signals to a communication satellite and can only be done by a trained installer. Moving locations means having the dish professionally re-installed (installation costs are usually under $150 in the U.S.).

Maximum required speed

If you need fast broadband service then you probably need two-way satellite service and, depending on the speed required, you may only have one or two vendors available.

The critical element is often upload speed, which is always slower than your download connection. A typical broadband subscription providing 500 Kbps download speeds will run about $55 per month in addition to about $500 for a one-time equipment purchase and installation. For another $20 per month you can have 1.5 Mbps download broadband with the same equipment. But the maximum upload performance will probably be limited to 256 Kbps even with the fastest download service. ❖

Are you a software snob? Ten hardware-centric assumptions that will eat into your sales

By Bruce Hadley, SoftwareCEO

In our frequent visits to the Inc. 500 list, we look for software company best examples; but, occasionally, we connect with some out-of-the ordinary surprises.

Case in point: We recently called on Enterprise Computing Solutions (ECS), because they were #62 on last year's list and #187 on the most recent Inc. roster of fastest-growing private companies in the U.S.

Founded in 1994, ECS, in 1997—the first year of its Inc. reporting—had 15 employees and $1.2 million in revenue. In 2002, sales were $33 million with 25 people; five-year revenue growth was 887 percent.

If you're in the software business, that headcount number probably tipped you off that ECS is not an ordinary ISV; their revenues-per-employee last year were $1.3 million, roughly 10 times what you'd expect from a software developer of their size.

In fact, Enterprise Computing Solutions is not a software developer; the Mission Viejo, CA, company is an implementer and hardware reseller for mission-critical systems.

From its own Web blurb: "ECS builds sophisticated IT infrastructure solutions for mission-critical applications, provides enterprise storage solutions that ensure data protection and business continuity, and delivers state-of-the-art server solutions for optimal computing capacity."

So, why feature ECS here? Because CEO David Butler engaged us in a spirited and highly instructional conversation about the software industry—from a hardware provider's point of view.

Admit it: At some point in your software career, you've made (or at least laughed at) a disparaging comment about the "box jocks" who provide the machines that host your software. Secretly or not, you've wondered whether hardware people are a few notches beneath you on the IT evolutionary scale.

Note

SoftwareCEO is the software industry's "Page One," with weekly tips and tactics from best-practices software firms, plus discussion forums, news, links, and online seminars. Site members also have access to downloads, proprietary research, and thousands of dollars in exclusive Buyers' Club discounts.

Well, listen up, boys and girls: Dave Butler is here to tell you that this kind of tunnel vision hurts you a lot more than it hurts him.

When faced with integrated systems deals—software, hardware, and services—here are ten common (and unfair) assumptions that software vendors make.

1. You think the deal is only about you.

"Most software vendors don't deal with a guy like me in their transactions," Butler says, "yet, in every one of their deals, there's a guy like me who can either work to their advantage or disadvantage.

"It's no different than any other sales cycle: You have to uncover all the points of influence that could impact your deal positively or negatively. There are going to be third-party points of influence that impact the deal—for example, a hardware infrastructure person—and that would be me.

"You'll have an implementation partner; you might have a leasing company involved in the deal—there are all these other parties out there providing input into the decision process. If the software sales force is pursuing the deal in a vacuum, it won't be by design, and it certainly won't be under your control. You're not managing your sales process and all its variables."

2. You think the hardware cost is trivial.

"Software people nearly always underestimate the hardware cost," Butler says. "They see it as just a black box.

"What I hear from the software guy is, 'Can you bring in some used equipment? And have it here by Monday?'

"Generally, our rule of thumb is that we take the simple advice that a software company gives, and triple their cost estimates. If it's a mission-critical situation, then the complexity and redundancy goes up again; the total is easily three to five times."

If it's a localized system with no special requirements, then 5 to 8 percent of the total budget will go to hardware, Butler says. But if it's a mission-critical install, figure on 25 percent.

"If you look at ERP systems, for example, the hardware requirements and costs for an SAP system can easily be 10 times greater than they are for a small- to medium-size business system.

"Our goal is to right-size the equipment. If we use the range of 5 to 25 percent of overall budget and come in with 12 percent, that's because we've studied it, analyzed the particular implementation—and because we've done it hundreds of times before."

3. You think the hardware effort is trivial.

There's more to the hardware side than unpacking boxes and plugging them in, Butler says, and ISVs typically underestimate the time required.

"Typically, the engineering timeframe involves 30 to 90 days to take the customer through all the variables they'll need to create their enterprise hardware strategy. Do you want Intel, do you want UNIX, or do you want Linux in the equation? All these things impact people and processes.

"If you came to me and said, 'I want a two-bedroom home,' as a real estate agent, I'd say that's not enough information. We could be talking about a $1 million condo overlooking the ocean, or we could be talking about a $100,000 mobile home.

"As a hardware provider, if I am to do a very good job with the customer, it will take 30 to 90 days to get through the process, and we will review five solid iterations.

"In addition, one of our jobs is to properly time-phase this, so that the executive knows from year to year what the total implementation is. They'll never get that from a software person."

4. You think the hardware guys are after "your" money.

"Too often, software vendors assume we're competing for the budget," Butler says. "But if we can get in there early enough to educate the customer, we're a value proposition to the customer.

"We get a lot of people who want to get a bill of materials and throw a bid in; that's not what we do. We can help properly position the budget: We can help set expectations based on the product you're looking for.

"My consultants are setting up criteria for decision processes between redundant servers; that kind of consulting isn't done by software companies. And, I don't do any implementation of software. There really is no overlap.

"Maybe this will sound naive, but I'm assuming we all want to do what's right for the customer." And, it goes without saying, software can't run without hardware.

5. You play favorites, often because you don't know any better.

Software vendors often find themselves recommending one brand of hardware over another, but these recommendations don't always reflect what's best for the end user.

For example, just because your software has been tested on the Acme Computers or you have a partnership with Acme, doesn't mean that the customer should necessarily install Acme's boxes.

"There are real strategic implications to different hardware choices," Butler says. "I'm an HP partner; if I'm fighting against IBM, I know it's against a very strong solution with equivalent value statements.

"If I'm competing against Sun, on the other hand, I know it's going to be more of a pricing battle. What we find is that there's zero education being done as to how to properly respond when it comes to hardware."

When software companies flub their hardware recommendations, it's usually unwittingly, Butler believes, because they don't know any better. But the reason they don't know any better is that, once again, they undervalue the hardware component.

6. You think all boxes are alike.

"Software people tend to think that a box is a box is a box," Butler says, "and, by the way, I do think that's true, at least to some degree.

"But, my space is mission critical: any application that is critical to your day-to-day operations you can't live without. I deal with a lot of very large companies, where they measure downtime in terms of dollars. In those situations, anyone who thinks boxes are all the same is hopelessly misguided.

"I've had situations where a system went down for three days due to pilot error. They didn't have a duplicate piece of equipment and process in place to catch that error—something we had recommended to them—and they're making $40 million in products a day, every day.

"Their decision to save $1 million on the system design cost them $5 million in losses a year later.

"The hardware may be the same, but the companies behind those boxes and their attitudes are very different. So, what's the mindset of the customer?

"If it's a Sun-oriented customer, we know it's going to be a difficult deal, and, in the end, there's going to be no margin in it. We'd campaign them very hard on what it takes to be mission critical."

7. You fail to capture their customer intelligence.

"We are one of the best sources for customer intelligence—and it's a two-way street," Butler says.

"If I'm not teamed with a software company—if I go into a customer and they say, 'Here are our finalists: JDE, SAP, and Oracle'—I'll say, 'Well, it's a lot of work to come up with a hardware plan for each; if you were to tell me whom to focus on, whom would it be?'

"Nine times out of 10, they'll tell me who they're leaning towards. And when I ask the customer why, they can be remarkably candid: 'I don't like the sales guy,' 'They blew the demo,' and so on.

"I can then call up my software friend and say, 'I don't think you've got the position you think you do.' Of course, the software guy could do the same thing: 'We run on HP and Sun and IBM; is there one you're leaning toward?'

"I don't want to make this sound underhanded, because it isn't—but if I was brought into a deal by Oracle, even if we're acting independently, I have a very strong interest in supporting that person and their sales effort.

"The rules of engagement are that you tend to protect your partner; otherwise, you find you don't have friends anymore."

8. You think only software people know how to sell.

"A lot of software guys tend to be pretty proud of themselves," Butler says. "They think of themselves as the best salespeople in the world, and they think of hardware people as stepchildren—as having skills below their own.

"I assure you, I've got the best people in the industry here. I've done $50 million with a Fortune 100 food company in five years. We have an entire methodology that we follow to close the deal, and our hit rate is four out of five; it's a very strong value proposition.

"I have people who sit in on all the meetings with that Fortune 100 company and talk about what software they're going to buy over the next two years. We know what they're going to buy, and what they're going to budget."

9. You fail to take to partnership initiatives.

"Software companies are really missing an opportunity for cooperative marketing," Butler says.

"If HP is doing a marketing effort, they might come to me and say, 'I want to focus on a Sun replacement program'—a rebate or spiff to get customers to switch. Why not include software in that equation?"

"I think there's a terrific opportunity here for alliances. Why doesn't HP partner with an Oracle or an SAP and target a market? Go after life sciences, say, and go to that niche with a complete solution. Customers don't care about your software; they care about solving their problem. Marketing to the business reasons is a much stronger message than attacking your competitor."

Hardware vendors' public policy is to never endorse one software provider over another, Butler says, "but, at a local level, there's nothing to stop people from getting together to do something."

"At the tactical level, it doesn't have to be as formal," Butler says. "For example, in L.A., I might put some marketing dollars in a regional campaign to join with HP to market a specific capability. If it works, then I'd do it in other territories, without making it into a formal national campaign."

Through hardware partnerships, you can "mobilize a virtual sales force of reps," Butler says. When you choose alliance partners, however, keep in mind that cozying up to one may hurt you with others. Therefore, Butler suggests, go with the numbers: In your market, do you have 40 HP reps and five from Sun? That would suggest you target HP and/or an HP-centric reseller.

Few software companies have the kind of clout to get the attention of hardware stalwarts HP, IBM, and Sun. If you follow Butler's train of thought, however, it may make sense to join forces with resellers like ECS who are strong in a particular region or market.

Hardware resellers typically get co-op dollars from the manufacturers equal to 0.5 percent of the reseller's sales, Butler says. "I get $100,000 to $200,000 a year from HP that I can use however I want.

"If I want, I could use some of that money to go to a software company and say, 'I've built a whole methodology to help you, and, oh, by the way, let's do some marketing—let's go out and target this segment together.'

"You need to define a target market that makes sense," Butler says. "If you're looking for someone who's more than just a broker or peddler, you need to discern whom you're talking to.

"Do they have the complete set of services you need to implement? Go to the manufacturer; go to HP and ask them who could do what you want the integrator and reseller to do. In Southern California, for example, there are 50 companies that can sell HP computers; but, when it comes down to what we do, there are only two.

"Identify the hardware company channel manager in each of the prospective geographies. In the Southwest, a guy named Mark Gerber at HP manages all the companies like me. He's responsible for knowing my value proposition, where I fit in, etc.

"His job is to represent the reseller's interests within HP; if HP's direct sales force needs a certain set of capabilities, he aligns those skill sets. He's a relationship manager. The only company that doesn't have channel managers is Dell, because theirs is a direct model."

10. You partner at the wrong level.

"It's best to build the relationship [with companies like ECS] at the sales manager-to-sales manager level," Butler says. "CEO-to-CEO friendships are fine, but that's at a much higher level, and that isn't where deals happen; deals happen at the street level.

"I would look for the regional managers and have a get-to-know-each-other event. We show up at your monthly sales meeting, do a 30-minute presentation on who we are, then go out for a soda pop afterwards.

"If we get involved with a software person, we will absolutely get involved with a process that maps into his needs, wants, and desires. We understand the motives of our partners, and I value the future reference.

"On the other hand, if the customer is working with a broker, there are going to be defensive plays; the hardware guy, if he's purely a broker, is going to work very hard to protect his turf."

There's a predictable pattern to ECS's partnerships with software companies, Butler says. "From day one, working with a software person who has no sensitivity to all these issues, they think we're competing for the dollars.

"But, as we start working with them—when we do five, six, or seven deals together—they'll start bringing us in from day one, because it's the surest way to not slow the deal down.

"We've now got a lot of converts. They know that by not working with the hardware partner, they can extend the deal by 30, 60, or 90 days, while I do the job I've got to do. By working together from the outset, I can help them wrap this deal up with a bow." ❖

10 things you should know about saving money on computer hardware

By Bill Detwiler, MCP

After personnel, equipment is often the second largest expense for an IT department. Saving money on hardware can have a significant impact on the bottom line, even for small and midsize organizations. Here are 10 real-life examples of how TechRepublic contributors and members are making the most of their hardware budgets.

1. Develop a written hardware policy.

Before you do anything else, your IT department should have a written hardware policy. This document doesn't have to be the Magna Carta, but it should outline all aspects of hardware standardization, purchasing, support, and acceptable use. A carefully planned and skillfully implemented policy should improve your IT department's efficiency, cutting down on unnecessary purchases.

2. Standardize equipment.

While not every user or department has the same needs, you should still standardize your equipment as much as possible. For example, TechRepublic employees have a choice of two laptops. Both are from the same manufacturer and have many interchangeable components: batteries, power supplies, hard drives, and docking stations. This practice increases troubleshooting efficiency and allows the IT department to purchase equipment in bulk and from a single vendor. This tip goes hand-in-hand with #3 and #4.

3. Buy in bulk.

Avoid purchasing single components or systems whenever possible. Manufacturers and retailers often offer discounts for large purchases. This may take more advanced planning, but the savings are worth it. TechRepublic contributor David Williams has found this technique to work especially well for blank storage media.

4. Use a single vendor.

This suggestion relates closely to #3. Using a single vendor helps develop bulk purchases, allowing you to exploit bulk-purchase discounts. Try to find a single vendor for all your server, workstation, and laptop needs. This will streamline equipment purchases, aid in standardization, and allow your organization to develop a long-term vendor relationship. I can say from personal experience that vendors treat long-standing clients better than the occasional buyer.

5. Use refurbished and hand-me-down equipment.

Ted Laun, a senior IS technician at TechRepublic, suggests using refurbished monitors if possible. Why pay full price for a new monitor when a refurbished one will work just as well? Training rooms, computer labs, community centers, and other locations where systems aren't used every day are perfect places for refurbished and hand-me-down equipment.

6. Make sure the user needs it.

Before buying that 19-inch LCD monitor or cutting-edge system, make sure the user actually needs the equipment. While your CAD designers may need the latest and fastest technology, most average users do not. Be critical of every request that comes across your desk. Unless the user can show a legitimate business reason for having a piece of equipment, don't buy it.

7. Limit laptop use.

Although laptop prices have declined, a laptop and docking station (with external monitor, keyboard, and mouse) are often significantly more than the purchase price of a regular desktop. Only provide laptops to employees who regularly work away from the office.

8. Choose peripherals carefully.

Contributor Michelle Hutchinson reminds us to use equipment appropriate for its work environment. Several of Michelle's users are in very dusty plants. Because of this, Michelle was constantly replacing mice. They finally switched to optical mice, which solved the problem. "I know it's on the lower end of money-saving ideas," Michelle said, "but it does add up."

9. Use alternative hardware solutions.

Michelle also suggests considering options other than standard PC systems. The same users mentioned in #8 switched to a thin client system on their assembly line because of the environment. "Upgrading every PC on the line was getting expensive," Michelle said. "By using thin clients connected to one server, we now upgrade one PC rather than 20."

10. Cut back on pagers.

Jeff Davis, a TechRepublic columnist who works for an application services provider, said his organization's office manager recently saved their company almost $900 a month by eliminating unnecessary pagers. Jeff's company provided pagers for many IT and non-IT employees. The office manager simply asked everyone with a company pager if they really needed it. Because most employees were also carrying personal or company-provided mobile phones, they discontinued service on nearly 40 percent of their pagers. ❖

10 things you should know about deploying a UPS

By Erik Eckel

Hurricanes, tornadoes, and earthquakes aren't the only disasters that damage PCs, servers, and other computers. The abrupt loss of electricity prevents systems from closing open applications, completing replication actions, finishing disk activities, and shutting down properly. Lost data and corrupted databases and applications often result.

Powerful electrical spikes also cause trouble. A computer's sensitive electronics can easily be destroyed by electrical surges spawned by lightning strikes or power grid fluctuations.

Uninterruptible power supplies (UPSes) help prevent the damage that occurs from both power loss and common electrical fluctuations. However, just plugging in a UPS and connecting computer equipment doesn't guarantee systems are properly protected. Keep these 10 items in mind to maximize the protection UPSes provide.

1. Data line protection is critical.

Computers connected to UPS devices still aren't protected from the ever-present risk of lightning strikes. Sure, the UPS may guard against the PC or server being damaged by electrical surges reaching the system via a power outlet, but lightning strikes just as easily travel telecommunications links, such as cable modem and DSL connections, to toast everything in their path (including motherboards and attached hardware).

Ensure that you configure your network properly. Install a UPS data protection circuit between your telecommunications provider's data line and your computer systems. Typically, the telecommunication circuit plugs in to a physical input on the UPS, which also presents an equivalent RJ-11 or RJ-45 outlet for continuing the circuit's connection to your local area network.

Should a strong electrical surge occur, the UPS's protective circuit will prevent the surge from destroying other equipment. The circuit may no longer function following such a strike, but replacing a UPS device is much less expensive than replacing multiple servers, PCs, and network switches.

2. Recovery software must be installed.

Often, it's tempting to just plug in a UPS, connect a computer or server, and get to work. Unfortunately, UPSes usually include proprietary software that must be installed for the unit to step in and properly power connected systems when the principal power source fails.

Always install a UPS's included software. In addition, be sure to connect the communications cable (typically USB or RS-232) to ensure that the PC or server and UPS can communicate.

3. Recovery software must be configured.

In addition to installing the proprietary software included with a UPS, you're best served configuring the program to meet your organization's specific needs. Although you can accept the manufacturer's default configuration, out-of-the-box settings may not allot sufficient time for shutting down a domain controller that must reconcile database, Active Directory, e-mail server, and other connections. Be sure that a system receives sufficient time to close all open connections and applications and properly shut down. Configuration options vary by manufacturer and model.

Review the default settings to determine whether they require adjustment. Often two options are available. You can specify either how long a system will run on batteries before initiating a shutdown sequence or you can specify that the UPS begin shutting down attached systems when its battery provides only enough power to operate for a certain number of minutes.

When configuring these settings, note that in both cases, the trigger focuses on initiating shutdowns based on battery values (either how long the battery's been running or how many minutes the battery can continue powering the current load). Regardless of which option you select, allow sufficient time for the shutdown sequence to complete. Some servers may require six, eight, or even 10 minutes to properly shut down; if the shutdown sequence is initiated when the battery possesses only five more minutes of power, data loss could result.

4. Batteries fail.

Batteries fail. It's a fact of life. Due to a completed lifecycle, manufacturer's defect, or some other cause, there's no guarantee a battery will operate as intended. Thus, even a high-quality UPS doesn't eliminate the need for ensuring data backups routinely complete properly.

Fortunately, UPS batteries typically provide warning signs that something's amiss. An online model may not properly power load levels, offline models may not test well, and still others may light warning or failure indicators. Regularly testing a battery helps ensure that it has sufficient capacity to power a system should the principal electricity source fail.

Regularly test a battery to make sure that it retains sufficient strength to power systems properly should the site's electrical supply fail. With systems supporting automated testing, schedule routine quick and deep cycle tests. Review the test logs regularly and keep an eye out for any anomalies that could indicate that failure is imminent. Always replace troubled batteries before they fail, as data loss could result if a failing battery remains in service.

5. Load levels change over time.

Think how your network has grown over time. New servers, workstations, and peripherals all place greater demand on UPS devices, but in most cases, the UPS was likely deployed with the original network—when power requirements were less.

Following expansion, be sure to recalculate the volts-amperes/wattage a UPS must provide. Whenever a server rack or workstation's equipment exceeds a UPS's capacity, either deploy an additional UPS or purchase a new model.

6. A UPS shouldn't power a laser printer.

Printing may prove a critical task, such as within billing or credit departments, but don't rely upon a UPS to power a laser printer. Even if the UPS is being used only to condition the electrical supply a laser printer receives, when attached to battery backup outlets on the UPS, laser printers quickly overpower a UPS and exceed standard load levels. The quickest way to generate multiple load level warnings and alerts (and potentially damage UPS electronics) is to power a laser printer using a UPS.

Why? A laser printer's fuser (which melts printer toner applied to paper) consumes a quick burst of energy. Most UPS models simply can't supply the required power as quickly as the laser printer demands.

7. Network connectivity is key in planning emergency power requirements.

When powering servers or even a workstation that serves as a workgroup server, it may be necessary to complete data replication, communications, or other activities requiring network connectivity when shutting down systems due to electrical outages. Thus, any network equipment between the systems performing the replication or data sharing must also receive power from UPS devices. If network switches, routers, firewalls, and any required telecommunications modems or routers don't also receive power from a UPS during an outage, the data replication and communications links will fail (and data loss could result).

8. Backups must terminate.

This is often a forgotten setting: Be sure to instruct Windows Backup (and third-party backup routines) to abandon backup operations if battery mode begins. Also, when using Windows' native backup utility, specify that the task not start if the system is running on batteries. Select the battery-related check boxes within Windows Backup's Power Management settings so that incomplete backups don't overwrite properly completed backups.

These settings are not Windows' default configuration. Unless a site experiences frequent power outages lasting just a few moments, consider entering the changes to prevent an incomplete or corrupt backup from overwriting a proper, previously completed backup file.

9. Service life is short.

The service life of a typical UPS battery is only a few years. UPS devices are often positioned on cubicle floors and behind desks. It's easy to forget they're there. Years can pass quickly.

As we mentioned in #4, batteries will eventually begin to fail. After a few years, batteries may continue to function but they likely won't continue providing the same levels of service. For example, a two-year-old battery may provide only 12 minutes of power versus 18 when it was new. Be sure to consider a battery's age and associated service degradation when reviewing your emergency power requirements.

Many UPS devices feature hot-swappable batteries. Such models enable changing a UPS' batteries without powering down attached equipment. Hot-swappable batteries are particularly useful when powering servers and other critical devices.

Thunderstorms, electrical sags and surges, and other conditions (including heat) can also shorten a UPS's service life. Ensure that a UPS receives a fighting chance at longevity by unplugging unused systems during storms, regularly checking battery strength, restricting load levels within reasonable limits, and keeping UPS products free of clutter (thereby giving them room to breathe and cool). If you do choose to unplug an unused UPS during thunderstorms, make sure that it's unused. In other words, verify that it's not protecting a telecommunications data circuit through which a lightning strike could travel and destroy connected equipment.

10. UPSes are lifeboats, not bridges.

When deploying UPS devices, never consider them bridges over troubled waters. Remember that UPSes are not generators. They're best used as lifeboats for escaping unexpected crises.

Although a UPS can certainly provide full functionality during a five-minute blackout, the devices shouldn't be used to bridge periods when electricity fails. Instead, if you view UPSes as a temporary solution for properly closing applications and processes and shutting systems down in an orderly manner, you're much less likely to suffer data loss, corrupted files and applications, and other failures as the result of blackouts. ❖

10 ways to protect systems from electrical catastrophes

By Erik Eckel

PCs, servers, switches, routers, broadband modems, KVM switches, and other computer equipment are all subject to electrical damage. From improper site wiring to lightning strikes, a wide variety of electrical issues threaten systems and peripherals constantly. Review these 10 items to ensure that you've taken necessary precautions to help protect against data loss and equipment damage.

1. Verify electricity levels.

Most computer equipment is designed to use 120 volts of AC power supplied at 60 hertz. Electrical current provided by a local utility or throughout a site or facility can vary from that standard, however, sometimes significantly.

When deploying new systems, and as facilities are expanded and adjoining sites grow, be sure the local power grid continues providing proper electrical baselines. Both sags and surges adversely affect PC and server electrical components and can lead to subsequent failures and data loss.

Use a multimeter to reveal the voltage an AC power outlet provides to systems and equipment. If baselines vary by two percent or less, invest in electrical conditioning equipment, such as an uninterruptible power supply (UPS). If baselines vary by three percent or more, contact the local utility, a licensed electrical contractor, or facilities management to explore and correct the errors.

2. Confirm that supply circuits are grounded properly.

Surge protectors and UPS devices can't properly safeguard the sensitive hardware they're designed to protect if the electrical outlets they're plugged in to aren't properly grounded. Ground wiring is responsible for diverting most power surges. When ground wiring is compromised, surges don't have an effective suppression path. Expensive servers, PCs, and network equipment can subsequently suffer significant damage.

Information technology professionals typically aren't responsible for a facility's wiring quality, but as they're responsible for maintaining the computer systems and networks powered by the facility's electrical supply, IT pros have an interest in ensuring electrical outlets and power supplies are properly grounded.

Many UPS and surge protector models will light a warning lamp if the outlet into which they're plugged isn't properly grounded. Most do-it-yourself and hardware stores also sell inexpensive circuit testers that are simply plugged in to outlets to confirm that circuits are grounded properly.

Whenever deploying new equipment, be sure to first test the circuit. When using surge protectors or UPS devices that feature improper-grounding alarms, also verify that the alarm light isn't lit.

3. Don't overload circuits.

Remember the *Christmas Story* scene in which Ralphie's dad blows a fuse connecting too many electrical plugs into a single outlet? In the popular holiday movie, a string of decorative lights is to blame, but too many desktop computers, servers, and network devices connected to a single *circuit* can easily overpower the electrical supply. Notice I didn't say too many desktop computers, servers, and network devices connected to a single *outlet.*

Splitting outlets (using power strips, surge protectors, and UPS devices), of course, does nothing but multiply the power demands placed upon the circuit to which those outlets are connected. Placing excessive demands upon a circuit can result in intermittent power failures, wide variations in available electricity, and even fire hazards as overworked circuits exceed safe operating ranges.

As CPU speeds and capacities and video card capabilities, among other elements, have increased, server and PC power requirements have grown as well. Carefully research your server room or office's power requirements to make sure the site's electricity requirements are sufficient.

Several resources are available for helping estimate appropriate power levels. Check out these sources for more information:

- "Calculating Total Power Requirements for Data Centers" (APC White Paper) http://www.apcmedia.com/salestools/VAVR-5TDTEF_R0_EN.pdf
- "Powering the Data Center Efficiently" (Hewlett-Packard White Paper) http://whitepapers.techrepublic.com.com/abstract.aspx?docid=92243&promo=400222&kw=%5c'calculate+power+requirements%5c'
- "System Power and Cooling Requirements" (Sun Microsystems Book Chapter) http://docs.sun.com/source/816-1613-14/Chapter4.html

4. Use a UPS/surge protector.

Avoid deploying unprotected power strips, which do nothing to protect connected equipment from sags, surges, and lightning strikes. Deploy surge protectors and UPS devices instead.

Connect all sensitive electronic equipment to UPS or surge protection devices. Remember that a laser printer's fusers generate strong bursts of electrical consumption that can damage UPS units.

Mobile systems pose a particular challenge. Ensure that all traveling employees carry and use effective surge protectors when traveling with laptops.

5. Properly calculate UPS/surge protector capacity.

Just as electrical circuits can easily be overwhelmed, so too can a UPS device's power capacity be exceeded. Carefully calculate the power demands for the systems attached to a UPS device to ensure that the UPS can power the connected equipment.

Most UPS manufacturers provide interactive calculators you can use to estimate the volts-amperes and watts required to power your systems. Use these links for more information:

- American Power Conversion Corp.'s product selection wizards
  http://www.apc.com/tools/ups_selector/index.cfm?lid=Go%20to%20the%20UPS%20Selector
- Belkin product selection wizards
  http://www2.belkin.com/config/surgeprotection/computersurgeprotection.asp
- Tripp Lite's product selectors
  http://www.advizia.com/tripplite/

When selecting surge protectors, purchase models featuring a sufficient number of protected outlets. A five-outlet surge protector may cover five devices, but it does no good if additional unprotected outlets must be utilized for other systems or peripherals.

Also ensure the surge protector selected includes lightning protection. Without protection from common thunderstorms, a surge protector can prove useless in safeguarding sensitive computer equipment from electrical spikes, resulting in failed hardware and corrupt and lost data.

6. Replace damaged or faulty UPS/surge protectors.

When a surge protector or UPS sustains a significant electrical surge, such as occurs with a lightning strike, the device's internal electronics can fail. If warning lamps light, outlets stop operating, or batteries fail, replace the damaged component or the entire UPS or surge protection device. You should do this even if the unit's telecommunications protective mechanism is the only component that fails.

Although it's tempting to continue using a UPS with only a single dead outlet or port, the fact the device sustained an electrical charge sufficient to damage components indicates that other damage may have occurred. Such damage could prevent the UPS or surge protector from properly protecting connected equipment, thus necessitating the device's replacement.

7. Protect telecommunications links.

Always make sure that servers, PCs, and network equipment receive protection from electrical spikes that can travel telecommunications links. Lightning strikes frequently discharge via cable modem, DSL, and telephone lines. The discharge isn't pretty, as everything from network interface cards to motherboards can be destroyed.

When purchasing UPS and surge protection devices, look for models that protect connected equipment from lightning strikes entering the network via data lines. Then, when deploying the UPS or surge protector, be sure to connect the data line to the protective device's input. Connect a corresponding RJ-11 or RJ-45 cable to the device's protected output to guard against lightning damage on your network.

8. Test power supplies.

Delicate electronic components within a computer, such as hard disk motors, memory, video cards, and motherboards, are sensitive to even minor fluctuations in a system's electrical supply. Even if circuits have been tested, proper grounding has been verified, and UPS or surge protectors are in place, a system's wayward power supply can inflict electrical damage on a PC or server.

Power supplies are a frequent cause of system reboots and failures. I've seen a power supply (on a system attached only to a power strip) continually reboot a machine while in the process of overheating. Thick, acrid white smoke poured from the malfunctioning power supply while the system kept repeating vain attempts to restart.

Whenever you encounter unexplained or intermittent reboots and other flaky behavior, check the power supply's electrical output to ensure it's working properly. Use either a multimeter, set to read the proper voltages, or a tool specifically designed to test a power supply's output.

Malfunctioning power supplies should be replaced immediately to protect a system's components from electrical damage and potential fire hazards. If a power supply has been distributing excessive electrical power to a system, it's not a bad idea to test the motherboard, CPU, memory, and other components using a POST card to make sure that no additional repairs are required.

9. Maintain proper operating temperatures.

Temperature is a well-known and well-documented enemy of network switches, firewalls, PCs, servers, and other equipment. High temperatures can adversely affect power supplies, potentially causing damage to a system's internal components. High temperatures can also prevent a UPS device's internal electronics from working properly, thereby leaving connected systems and equipment at risk.

Protect against electrical damage resulting from overheating by ensuring that systems receive proper cooling. Keep all vents and fan outlets free of debris, boxes, files, folders, and other furniture. When performing routine system maintenance, verify that PC and server exhaust fans are working properly and are unobstructed.

I've encountered situations in which a PC's exhaust fans were blocked by documentation placed inside the system (to prevent the discs and license numbers from becoming separated from the unit or being lost). A good idea in theory, but the resultant ventilation loss prompted the hard disk to fail as a result of its baking in the heat generated by its own electrical activity.

Take steps to ensure that UPS devices also receive ample room to breathe. Don't stack boxes, retired PCs, or other equipment alongside UPSes, either in server rooms or in cubicles.

Electricity use consistently generates heat, and that heat must be dissipated properly or damage and potential data loss will result. It sounds simple, but take a quick walk through any office environment and you'll almost always find at least one UPS buried by boxes, files, or other office material.

10. Maintain proper insurance.

You can take numerous steps to prevent electrical damage to computers, servers, and other computing equipment, but sometimes your best efforts simply aren't sufficient. I've seen clients lose motherboards, NICs, hard disks, and more due to lightning strikes. Some of the damaged equipment was even connected to UPS and surge protectors.

Despite precautions, equipment can still end up being lost to electrical damage resulting from surges, lightning, and other disturbances. Business owners, even those with small operations, should make sure that insurance policies include riders or passages expressly covering computers and associated equipment. IT professionals employed by larger organizations should also work with their CTOs to properly maintain documentation required by the corporation's insurers.

Review your organization's property and casualty insurance policies. SOHO operators should review homeowner's policies. Regardless of organization size, you should record the model numbers, serial numbers, and purchase prices of all equipment. Also, collect photographs of all computer and related items. Both the insurance policies and the supporting documentation should be securely stored off site. If a devastating electrical crisis does occur, having proper insurance and associated documentation can help your organization recover much more quickly and efficiently. ❖

10 things to seek in an uninterruptible power supply/surge-protection device

By Erik Eckel

Disasters come in all shapes and sizes. One of the most common, and sometimes most debilitating to businesses, is the lightning strike. Electrical spikes wreak havoc on servers, PCs, broadband modems, printers, switches, routers, and other equipment.

Thunderstorms spawn a host of tech support calls. An office or home need not even experience a direct strike to suffer crippling damage. I've encountered situations in which a tree's been struck by lightning and the subsequent electrical charge followed a nearby buried telephone line into a home office, fried an answering machine and PCI fax/modem card, traveled through the motherboard (leaving it unscathed) on its way to destroying the system's video card. I've also repaired client systems where a PC's power supply, RAM, and video card were rendered inoperable and the motherboard's capacitors were blown but the hard drive continued to operate without trouble.

In fact, a lightning strike need not even occur. Power sags, brownouts, and blackouts can all lead to unintended shutdowns and data loss. Surges and poorly conditioned power feeds, too, can cause sensitive electronic components to fail.

Fortunately, uninterruptible power supplies (UPS) provide safeguards against most all of these threats, while surge protectors offer an economical defense against many forms of electrical spikes. Here are 10 features to review when purchasing a UPS or surge protector.

1. Power capacity

When reviewing UPS options, volts-amperes/wattage should be the first consideration (volts-amperes/wattage indicates a device's power capacity). An underpowered UPS can't properly prevent data loss resulting from unintended shutdowns. For that reason, it's critical that a UPS be matched well with the power loads it must support.

APC, a leading vendor of UPS devices, recommends deploying a UPS boasting a minimum of 510 volt-amperes (VA) and 357 watts to support a common Dell PowerEdge 1850 1U server setup and a 14-inch LCD. APC's 1000 VA/600 watt rackmount/tower UPS could operate such a setup for an estimated 15 minutes.

Small businesses using a tower PC as a workstation server (with a 15-inch LCD) might select a 350VA/200 watt UPS. With that power capacity, the small business could expect the UPS to power the system for approximately six minutes, or long enough to complete a proper shutdown.

When calculating your network's electrical requirements, be sure to account for additional equipment and peripherals that must continue operating, at least for a short period, during an outage. Examples of such easily forgotten equipment include external hard disks, KVM switches, storage area network appliances, and routers and switches enabling servers to complete communications before shutting down.

2. Outlet capacity

UPS devices, of course, provide power outlets that supply electricity to computers and peripherals when the main electrical supply fails. Many UPS models also feature surge-protected outlets that protect connected equipment from damaging spikes.

Technology professionals typically calculate the number of required battery backup outlets properly, as the UPS device's main purpose is to power the systems attached to them. The number of surge-protected outlets needed is easily overlooked.

The number of power outlets a UPS (and surge protection device) possesses is quickly exceeded, so be sure to review your current network setup before purchasing a UPS. Don't forget to allow for broadband modem, switch, firewall, KVM, and external hard disk power supplies in calculating the total number of required surge-protected outlets.

3. Electrical protection

Computers and related peripherals are typically designed to receive 120 volts of AC power at 60 Hertz. The actual electricity a wall outlet provides, however, can vary significantly from that baseline.

Surge protectors regulate the power quality supplied to computers and peripherals, while many UPS models actually tune and condition the electricity they supply to attached equipment. Surge protectors also block voltage levels exceeding specific thresholds (as do UPSes). High-quality surge protectors (and UPSes) even prevent damage occurring from lightning strikes. Be sure to review a UPS/surge protector's technical specifications to ensure the device protects against lightning damage; if a model does not cover lightning strikes, continue searching for one that does.

When a surge protector or UPS sustains a particularly powerful spike, the protector's internal mechanisms can be damaged. Subsequently, the unit may no longer function correctly, thereby leaving connected equipment subject to damage from future spikes and surges. Seek models that include failsafe technologies in the event that internal mechanisms become compromised. Some models disconnect equipment attached to failed outlets, while other brands may include warning lights.

Field experience demonstrates that surge protectors, in particular, frequently surrender their operational lives in saving attached equipment from destruction. But it's not always possible to know that a protective power strip is no longer functioning properly. Thus, such failsafe technology proves critical.

4. Data line protection

Gone are the days of just protecting computers and monitors from electrical spikes. Broadband links and even dial-up fax/modems (in servers, PCs, and laptops) provide common inroads for destructive electrical spikes.

If a computer is connected to a powerful UPS, but an associated DSL, cable, telephone, or other telecommunications circuit goes unprotected, even the most potent UPS can prove worthless. While the computers themselves might be protected from direct spikes, it's incredibly easy (and common) for lightning strikes to discharge through a cable modem, DSL, or other telecommunications link. Once in a network, the indirect damage can prove devastating as the spike travels Ethernet cables and toasts everything in its path, including network switches, NICs, motherboards, video cards, routers, and more.

I've seen it happen, and colleagues even report removing black-singed Ethernet cables from systems. Avoid such occurrences by selecting a UPS that offers data line lightning protection.

5. Bundled software

The software bundled with a UPS often makes the difference between a UPS serving as a simple protective mechanism versus a sophisticated data reporting device. While a UPS's job is to condition the power supply provided by a local utility for use by sensitive electronic equipment and to provide emergency power when the main electrical supply fails, higher quality uninterruptible power supplies also include sophisticated software.

Such software can report the electricity supply's condition, including input and output voltage, input and output frequencies, and load levels. Strong software also enables supporting network connectivity to a UPS and alarm configuration (as I'll discuss in greater detail shortly).

Most UPSes also include an application that enables specifying actions to take if the power sags or fails. Many organizations can't monitor PCs and servers 24/7, so programming a UPS to automatically shut down an attached PC or server proves more than convenient; it can mean the difference between corrupting a database and losing information or properly shutting down database, file, and mail servers with no data loss.

A SOHO should require such software be included with any UPS it purchases. Large organizations, meanwhile, may have more sophisticated fault-tolerant systems in place, but many may choose to leverage the UPS-provided application to properly shut down systems.

6. Equipment protection warranty

It seems like a no-brainer, but warranties vary widely. When purchasing a surge protector or UPS, review the manufacturer's equipment protection warranty and any applicable limitations. Always register a surge protector or UPS the day it's deployed, too; otherwise, collecting reimbursement should damage occur could prove impossible.

7. Alarm capabilities

UPS devices possessing the appropriate software can report when thresholds for a number of values, including voltage fluctuations, brownouts, blackouts, loading levels, operating temperatures, and battery strength, are exceeded. In addition to audible tones, alarms can be configured to send administrators e-mail messages if specified thresholds are exceeded. These alarms can prove invaluable in alerting users that problems are afoot, as potentially damaging power fluctuations don't always result in more attention-getting outages.

8. UPS type

UPSes essentially leverage two operating technologies: offline and online. The difference relates to the way a UPS powers attached equipment.

Typically, a UPS receives electricity from a wall outlet powered by a local energy utility. The utility-supplied electricity is converted from AC to DC by a rectifier inside the UPS device. The rectifier's DC power then passes to an inverter (which is connected to the actual computer equipment the UPS protects and powers) and a series of batteries. In some models a flywheel substitutes for batteries. When the utility-supplied electricity fails, battery power (or a flywheel) kicks in to supply the energy the inverter distributes to attached equipment.

Standby models, often referred to as offline devices, don't continually engage the system's battery. Instead, standby UPSes tap battery power only when electrical outages occur. They transfer operation from utility to battery power so fast, though, that a PC typically continues operating until it's shut down or the UPS runs out of juice. Occasionally, even a short sub-100 millisecond delay in switching power sources can cause hiccups and potential data loss. Offline models tend to cost less than line-interactive devices.

With online (also known as line-interactive or continuous) models, the battery continuously provides the electricity used by the inverter to power equipment attached to the UPS device. The battery is continuously charged as the device operates. Should the principal electrical source fail, the battery continues providing electricity until its charge depletes. Line-interactive models provide a cleaner and more consistent energy source than standby models and consequently cost much more.

If you're operating within a SOHO environment, a standby model will likely meet all your needs. In mission-critical environments or larger enterprises, line-interactive models are typically required.

9. Network manageability

UPS features vary by model and manufacturer. When researching a UPS for your organization, remember that accessing the device's configuration settings, status menus, and system logs is simplified when the UPS can be accessed remotely via an Ethernet network.

Less expensive UPS models typically require accessing the system locally (using the system to which the UPS is attached) to view system configuration, various alarm parameters, and system logs. In server rooms with multiple PCs, servers, and UPS devices, linking to each UPS locally quickly proves impractical.

10. Visual battery replacement indicator

Possibly the most underappreciated feature of any UPS is a battery warning light. The simple warning indicator alerts even casual users to failed or dying batteries.

The worst time to discover a battery requires replacing is when the power goes out. That's often when many users learn the lesson the hard way. No one should have to rebuild a report, recreate a PowerPoint presentation, or recover a corrupted e-mail database from a backup as a result of a UPS failing to provide sufficient time to shut down a system properly.

Although server room UPS devices tend to be more attentively monitored and tested, it's not uncommon for SOHO-deployed units to simply be forgotten. Receiving a visual indicator that a battery requires replacement, however, can help prevent battery failures (and the subsequent chain of failed events they fuel) before they occur. ❖

Notes:

Web Development

10 things every Perl hacker (and expert) should know

By Chad Perrin

Perl is the expert system administrator's scripting language of choice, but it is also a lot more than that. As a language designed for file and text processing, it is ideally suited to UNIX system administration, Web programming, and database programming, among dozens of other uses.

As one of the easiest programming languages to use for whipping up quick, effective code for simple tasks, Perl attracts new users easily and has become an important and popular tool for getting things done. Before jumping fully into Perl programming, though, there are a few things you should know that will make your life easier, both when writing code and when asking for help from Perl experts.

1. Perl is not an acronym.

Perl is sometimes known as the Practical Extraction and Report Language, because it's very practical and it is very good at extracting data and creating reports using that data. It is also known humorously as the Pathologically Eclectic Rubbish Lister, for reasons that might become obvious after you've used it for a while. Both of these phrases are equally "official" and equally correct, but the language is not PERL. It was named Perl before either of those phrases was invented, and the language is in fact not technically an acronym at all. When speaking of the language, call it Perl, and when speaking of the parser (the interpreter/compiler), it is acceptable to call it perl, because that is how the command used to run it is spelled. One of the quickest ways to get identified as a know-nothing newbie when talking to Perl hackers is to call it PERL.

2. There is more than one way to do it.

One of the main mottos of the Perl language and community is TIMTOWTDI, pronounced "Tim Toady." This one really is an acronym, and it stands for There Is More Than One Way To Do It. It's true of Perl on many levels and is something important to keep in mind. While some ways to do something are often better than other ways to do the same thing, you can be sure that for pretty much everything you can do with Perl, there is more than one way to do it.

3. Use warnings and use strict.

Warnings and the strict pragma are important weapons in the Perl hacker's arsenal for debugging code. (A pragma, in Perl, is a preprocessor directive. In other words, it's an instruction sent to the compiler before the code is compiled for execution.

Pragmas change how the compiler parses code.) Warnings will not prevent a program from executing, but will give helpful information on how the code can be fixed up.

The strict pragma will actually prevent the code from executing if a strict approach to programming style is not used, such as lexically scoping variables. Once in a while, a program might be better off without the strict pragma, but if you're new to Perl it will surely be a long time before you learn to recognize such situations, and until then you should just use it.

A Perl script with warnings turned on in the shebang line and the strict pragma used, on a standard UNIX system, would start like this:

```
#!/usr/bin/Perl -w
use strict;
```

Warnings can also be turned on with a `use` statement, like this:

```
#!/usr/bin/Perl
use strict;
use warnings;
```

4. Use taint checking.

With the *-T* option on the shebang line of your program, you explicitly turn on taint checking. This is a security measure that checks all input for your program for "tainted" data, to help ensure that incoming data will not allow arbitrary code execution if a malicious user is trying to crack security on the system running your code. This is especially important in circumstances where you are using Perl/CGI scripts to process data from an HTML form on the Web. It can be combined with the *-w* option as *-wT*.

5. Use lexically scoped variables.

You can use the *my()* operator to create variables using lexical scoping. In brief, this means that the scope of the variable is limited to the current context: if you declare a variable using *my()* inside a subroutine, the variable only exists inside that subroutine. The value of lexical scoping is that it protects different parts of modular code from one another.

For instance, if you're using a Perl module or library without knowing exactly what the code inside it looks like, using lexical variables can help to prevent accidentally assigning new values to variables that need to remain unchanged until later. It is especially important to use lexical scoping for your variables when writing modules and libraries in Perl. For those coming to Perl from other languages, you may know of the concept of lexically scoped variables as "private variables."

6. Name your programs properly.

Perl programs should have the appropriate file extension in their names. Many lower-quality Perl howtos simply use the *.pl* extension for everything, naming Perl scripts something like *foo.pl*. Technically, the *.pl* extension should be used for Perl libraries, not for executable Perl programs. For executable files, you should either use *.plx* or, if your operating system will allow it, no file extension at all. Perl modules, meanwhile, should use the *.pm* file extension. It is also considered good practice to use only alphanumeric characters and underscores in Perl script filenames, and to start those filenames with a letter (or underscore), similar to how you would start variable names.

7. Take advantage of CPAN.

The Comprehensive Perl Archive Network (CPAN) is a rich resource for finding freely available, reusable code. In particular, CPAN is where you'll find legions of Perl modules that can be used to enhance the functionality of your programs and reduce the time you spend writing them. The options you have for using CPAN vary from one operating system and Perl parser implementation to the next, but you can always browse CPAN using your Web browser (**http://search.cpan.org/**). Perl implementations generally come with at least a command-line tool for installing Perl modules from CPAN.

8. Know how to use Perldoc.

The online documentation for Perl is extensive and comprehensive, in the form of Perldoc. With Perldoc installed on your system, you can use it to access documentation on any of the standard Perl functions, installed modules, variables, and a slew of other things—even Perldoc itself! It's like having one of the most complete programming reference books available right at your fingertips, for free, and searchable since it's in electronic format.

On some systems, Perldoc will be installed by default with Perl itself, and on others the process for installation should be self-evident. If you have problems getting Perldoc installed, you can always access the online Perldoc Web site. Make sure you know how to use Perldoc, because it can make you a more effective Perl hacker in ways that just might surprise you.

9. Don't reinvent the wheel.

You should use subroutines, modules, and libraries often. (The term "subroutine" in Perl means roughly the same thing as "function" in C.) The point is to help you write code faster and keep that code from becoming unmanageable if you need the same functionality in multiple programs or more than once in the same program. This is accomplished by separating blocks of code from the rest of your source code using subroutines, modules, and libraries. You're better off using a design for the wheel that already exists, rather than reinventing the wheel from scratch, most of the time. In addition, when you're reusing code from a subroutine, module, or library and you need to improve that code somehow, you only need to change it in one place.

10. Regular expressions are your friends.

Perl's regular expression syntax can help to make your source code look intimidating to the uninitiated, and as a result sometimes people new to Perl programming avoid regexen (http://techrepublic.com.com/5100-3513-5951500.html). (Often Perl hackers and other programmers who use regular expressions will refer to them as "regexen" or "regexes" in the plural ("regex" singular). An alternate version of "regex" is "regexp," though why anyone would want to add that extra letter, making it more difficult to pronounce clearly, is beyond me.) This is, really, a mistake. Regular expressions add a great deal of power to the Perl programming language, often allowing the programmer to do something in three lines that might otherwise take 50 lines of code. Regular expressions are expressions made up of abbreviations for matching patterns in strings that can be used to find and manipulate smaller strings inside larger strings. It behooves the Perl hacker to learn regex syntax and learn it well.

Once you've internalized the lessons of this list, you're ready to really start learning Perl and how to program with it. Some good resources for beginners (and experts, too) include Learning Perl (http://www.amazon.com/gp/product/0596101058/sr=8-1/qid=1142482296/ref=pd_bbs_1/104-0450629-6672717?%5Fencoding=UTF8) for an excellent introductory text, the PerlMonks (http://www.perlmonks.org/) community for tutorials and discussion, and Ovid's CGI Course (http://users.easystreet.com/ovid/cgi_course/) for Perl/CGI Web programming. ❖

10 most useful Perl developer modules for cryptography and authentication

By Melonfire

As the World Wide Web and the applications it supports become ever more pervasive, online security is becoming more and more important. Encryption and authentication are now *de riguer* on most Web sites, and users demand strong security from the tools they use.

If you're a Perl application developer (http://techrepublic.com.com/5264-1-0.html?query=perl), you're—thanks to the Comprehensive Perl Archive Network (CPAN)—already ahead of the pack. This is because CPAN has numerous ready-made Perl modules to enable developers to efficiently perform common tasks related to application security, user authentication, and data encryption. This document, points you to ten of the most important ones, describes how they are used, and provides you with a link so that you can get started.

> **Note:**
>
> You can install CPAN (http://www.cpan.org/misc/cpan-faq.html#How_install_Perl_modules) directly from the Internet, by following the instructions provided on their Web site.

1. Crypt::GPG

This module provides an API to encrypt, sign, and decrypt files using public/private key authentication with the GNU Privacy Guard. It uses an object-oriented interface to generate new key pairs, manipulate the key database, or verify signed files.

Use this module when you need to create or perform GnuPG encryption or decryption in a Perl application.

2. Crypt::Blowfish

This module provides an object-based interface to encrypting and decrypting test using the Blowfish encryption algorithm.

Use this module when you need to encrypt sensitive data (such as passwords) using the Blowfish algorithm.

3. Crypt::RSA

This module provides an object-based interface to encrypt, sign, and decrypt files using RSA public/private key authentication. The API includes methods to generate new keys and verify signatures.

Use this module when you need to encrypt e-mail or files using public/private key authentication.

4. Crypt::IDEA

This module provides an object-based interface to encrypting and decrypting test using IDEA block cipher encryption.

Use this module when you need to encrypt sensitive data (such as passwords) using IDEA encryption.

5. Digest::MD5

This module provides a Perl interface to create MD5 message digests of files or string sequences.

Use this module when you need to generate MD5 "fingerprints" of a file or string.

6. Crypt::SaltedHash

This module provides an object-based API for one-way encryption with a "salt" or seed value. This technique is similar to that used in *NIX password files.

Use this module when you need to protect a string with one-way encryption or test the contents of an encrypted string.

7. Crypt::PassGen

This module provides an API to create pronounceable passwords from a dictionary. It works by building a frequency file from the dictionary and using that information in the password-generation process.

Use this module when you need to generate pronounceable usernames or passwords that are easy to remember.

8. Authen::PAM

This module provides an object-oriented interface to the Linux Pluggable Authentication Module (PAM), a versatile mechanism for user authentication. It can be used to access, verify, and modify user credentials, set and read environment variables, and work with PAM user sessions.

Use this module when you need to interface with the Linux authentication system through a Perl application—for example, to alter a user's password.

9. Authen::Users

This module provides a framework to manage and authenticate users with a password database (MySQL or SQLite). It includes a number of well-thought-out functions designed to manage users, organize users into groups, and manipulate the relationship between groups and group members.

Use this module if your Perl applications need a simple password database to manage user/group accounts.

10. Authen::PIN

This module is designed to create cryptographically strong numeric sequences from user-supplied templates. Internal verification digits (based on checksums), counters, and literals are all supported.

Use this module when you need to create a hard-to-guess numeric PIN or a number sequence that supports internal verification. ❖

10 things you should do to plan an effective portal initiative

This list is based on the article "Planning portal initiatives: Ten steps to success" (http://techrepublic.com.com/5100-10878 11-5449649.html) by Brian Hazzard.

As the Internet has increasingly been used to connect people, information, and applications, companies have raced to support business units and customers with online solutions. But many such solutions—corporate sites, extranets, intranets, self-service applications, and the supporting infrastructure—have been developed in discrete initiatives utilizing a host of technologies. Maintaining these "siloed" initiatives is costly, and controlling the aggregate customer experience has become increasingly difficult. As a result, the solution may not be meeting the needs of employees, partners, customers, or suppliers—putting loyalty, productivity, and revenue at risk.

Portals have gained popularity because they address these issues. Planned and implemented well, a portal provides a single point of access to diverse sets of information and applications. However, many portal initiatives fail during implementation or quickly fall into disuse. Portal initiatives are complex, but the reasons for failure (or success) are universal. The following 10 steps outline the requirements for planning a successful portal initiative.

1. Establish your objectives.

Is this an internal portal, or intranet; a public portal; or private extranet? Is it part of a larger effort to integrate multiple sites and/or applications or are there other reasons? Your answers will guide choices of architecture, technology, and design. Then, determine the business goals you expect to achieve with the portal. Common goals include:

- Reduced operational costs
- Increased productivity
- Improved decision-making
- Stronger business relationships
- Streamlined business processes
- Increased customer satisfaction

2. Build your business case.

Before starting a portal effort, build your business case. Failure to identify business objectives and success criteria can lead to failure, even before you begin. Often the assumptions behind the business plan ultimately define the success criteria for the portal initiative. Frequently, internal portals focus on increasing operational efficiency, while external portals concentrate on increasing market share, revenue streams, and customer retention.

Next, estimate the cost of the initiative. Before selecting a platform, understand the user experience, integration options, and security solutions that are required. Consider the full range of expenses, including licensing, training, design, development, testing, and maintenance costs. Costs should be revisited once the platforms are identified and a plan is established, when the investment required may be more accurately anticipated. Finally, consider reevaluating your approach after building the business case. Ask yourself: Is this portal needed? What is the potential ROI?

3. Plan a phased approach.

Since portals generally integrate a number of applications, these initiatives tend to be highly transactional and commonly incorporate advanced security features. Don't expect to get every feature into your first release. Rather, plan a phased project—focused on the highest priority business scenarios first—to ensure initial success. Once the most critical transactions are identified, concentrate subsequent iterations on advanced scenarios and features.

4. Establish a governance structure.

Because portals integrate assorted experiences and applications from dispersed business units, there can be governance issues across the enterprise. Clarity around decision-making is critical. For example, if Customer Relations owns the CRM application and Human Resources owns the intranet, what is the process for deciding what to integrate and what to link out of the portal? Establish and secure the resources required to support the initiative. Without support from the top down, the portal initiative will always be at risk.

5. Invest in training.

If a commercial portal product is chosen, realize that portal infrastructures provide a different way of architecting solutions. To efficiently leverage the platform's capabilities, you need a solid understanding of how the portal platform works. So training should be scheduled once the platform is selected.

To gain experience with the portal technology, consider creating a proof of concept. The proof of concept may be structured to mitigate high-risk areas and/or to validate design or user experience. This step should be taken early in the process, both to validate your technical approach and to allow stakeholders to envision what they are ultimately going to get. Finally, the initial implementation should set standards for the user experience and the technical implementation that should be followed as future portlets are integrated with the application.

6. Establish the infrastructure.

Infrastructure delays can frequently impede projects. These complexities often impose requirements on the network architecture, content management, database connectivity, application communications, and security infrastructure. Plan the portal development and runtime environments early on, possibly as distinct phases that are managed accordingly.

7. Design the user experience.

The "behind the scenes" work of various applications integrated by the portal should be invisible to the user, no matter how complex. Prior to the design phase, ask:

- What user segments do you want to engage?
- What are the main tasks they'll perform?
- How will the portal affect productivity?
- Have the project goals been reconciled against the costs?

The answers to these questions are key to a compelling, cost-effective experience. Common tools used to ensure a successful user experience include usability testing, personas, user surveys, task analysis, card sorting, and taxonomies.

8. Clarify content management infrastructure.

Although the goal is an integrated and seamless front end, portal content is often managed by dispersed business units, each with disparate development and workflow requirements. In many legacy applications, a simple content change requires a striking amount of lead time; this is in direct conflict with the notion that portal success is measured by its ability to deliver timely information and services. Content management systems can address this pain, providing business units with greater control over content and allowing nontechnical users to manage content using familiar desktop tools.

Since portal infrastructures require consistent, well-categorized content to target relevant information for the user, many portal products feature integrated content management technology. The ideal scenario is to service the varying system requirements using a common platform. To this end, content management should be an enterprise-wide effort that facilitates the many content needs of your portal application.

9. Identify security needs.

Portals generally require security services such as confidentiality, integrity, and availability. Because portals integrate multiple applications, single sign-on (SSO) is often critical for a successful user experience, as it provides security across applications using a single authentication request. Ask:

- Is there an existing security framework?
- Will the portal be accessed from multiple locations and devices, with different security requirements and capabilities?
- Will it integrate with services provided by external partners with different security policies and integration requirements? The answers to these questions will determine whether the portal platform provides the necessary infrastructure to meet your security requirements.
- Must your portal integrate with sensitive external applications?

10. Invest in testing.

Portal projects bring together a large amount of functionality. If managed improperly, integration may result in unexpected and complex issues, such as contention for system resources. Define test cases early and plan for extensive user testing to ensure a scenario that works across the enterprise. With technology advancements that have vastly improved portal products, a portal can be a sound business investment. However, organizations evaluating portals should understand the complexities beyond technology. Because the technology frequently integrates a diverse set of content and services, portal initiatives tend to cross organizational boundaries and involve multiple stakeholders with differing business objectives. Success is determined by how well the portal is planned—and later, by the extent it is utilized. Taking the steps outlined in this article will help you prepare for this potentially rich and rewarding journey. ❖

10 things you should know about Microsoft's Visual Studio 2005 Team System

By Scott Robinson

Everybody talks about collaborative development tools (http://whitepapers.techrepublic.com/abstract.aspx?docid=66710), and heaven knows you can't surf the major developers' Web sites for 10 minutes without getting hit by banners trumpeting the latest. We can't fault Microsoft for wanting a piece of that action; but we need more than just a collaborative environment. For most IT shops, collaborative development is something in the future, something not yet being done. What is needed is a collaborative solution that:

- is tightly integrated with tools already in use
- is highly intuitive, and
- offers a new development methodology that doesn't represent abandonment of every process already in place.

Visual Studio Team System is Microsoft's response (http://techrepublic.com.com/5138-3513-5955502.html). The concept is very articulately defined, the up-side being that it will provide all the structure a team might require, all the tracking tools needed to manage the effort, and all the tools for every collaborative purpose. The down-side is that Microsoft is once again going several steps too far in deciding how we should do things. Will it work for your team? It's well worth a look. For myself, I'm hoping it gets a serious audition in my current assignment, since the collaborative tools in place at the moment aren't getting the job done by a long shot.

The concepts driving Team System need some fairly elaborate exposition in and of themselves and aren't undertaken here: instead, here's an overview of noteworthy features—some new and innovative, and some expected but improved—to stir your thinking on Team System as a possible direction for your shop.

1. Architectural diagrams

IT developers (and managers and executives) write this word on your foreheads: *ARCHITECTURE*. The single biggest missing link in IT development today, platform aside, is the lack of proper architectural thinking in application development. This is why the world makes jokes about us involving woodpeckers.

There are far, far too many nuts-and-bolts geniuses out there who can rewrite DaVinci's Codex in T-SQL, but who think two-dimensional client-server architecture is good enough for Internet apps. To build decent apps today, and Internet apps in particular, you need more than an idea, more than good tools, more than an application-level design; you need an application architecture, a high-level framework that carefully addresses your applications' intended functionality within the context of your hardware, network, and data-source infrastructure—and, worse yet, too many IT managers who know the buzzwords but don't yet really understand this. Too many IT development teams crash and burn, becoming full-time firefighters, because increasing user traffic chokes their database access to nothing, and because their apps simply can't be modified and enhanced within timeframes acceptable to their users.

Team System is addressing this shortfall in its Team Edition for Software Architects with a tool called Application Designer, a graphical workhorse for solution architecture. It enables users to create diagrams of application system solutions including many components of different types (i.e., apps, Web services, interfaces) and generate skeletal code in your language of choice (note that the Team Edition for Software Developers gives you the diagramming capability but not the code-generating capability). The diagram defines the connections between diagram components and allows you to constrain them as needed.

The idea (and it's a good one) is to address the different developmental needs of the architect, as opposed to the needs of managers and developers. The architect's toolkit gets more here than it is usually given, built on the VS/TS concept of "distributed application diagrams." This kit strives to capture all of the process, not just the workflow and coding, and includes architectural diagramming tools for System diagrams, Application diagrams, Deployment diagrams, and Logical Datacenter diagrams (more on this last one below).

2. Leveraging the Microsoft Solutions Framework 4.0

The Microsoft Solutions Framework 4.0 (http://whitepapers.techrepublic.com/abstract.aspx?docid=86342) (MSF) describes methodologies by which application development can be planned and implemented according to best practices. Version 4.0 is implemented in Team System and provides you with two ready-to-go system development life cycle (SDLC—http://techrepublic.com.com/5100-10878_11-5790009.html) models, one for agile development and one for process improvement.

The implementations of these methodologies, Microsoft hastens to point out, are prescriptive; that is, they are not simply generalized methodologies implemented for the sake of giving you general pointers, but are instance-specific, giving your team specific action guidance based on the particulars of the application you are implementing.

Created very much with team activity in mind, MSF 4.0 provides a meta-model mechanism for detailed methodology development and implementation, put into practice by an advocacy group (fancy term for team + interested parties). Such an ambitious jump can't be perfect, and we don't expect it to be, but it's a step in the right direction, especially for an IDE software solutions provider that is notably non-agile.

3. Team role definitions and constraints

The MSF implementation invokes a Team Model that assigns all project participants a role, or combination of roles, upon which a project participant's tasking, privileges, responsibilities, and constraints are based. In Team System, these roles include Project Manager, Architect, Developer, Tester, and the optional roles of Release Manager and Business Analyst.

Perhaps the single biggest consequence of a team member's role as defined in Team System is the edition of Team System they will use, which by definition constrains what they physically can and cannot do within a project or development effort. Other consequences of role include project permissions (which also enable and constrain) and advocacy assignment.

4. Project/Excel integration

Not long ago, I tried to argue a project manager into giving Microsoft Project a try. "Show me something Project can do," he replied, "that Excel can't." My response, which was not at all brief, will wait for another day—because, whether you're a Project manager or an Excel manager, Team System will accommodate you.

The Team Foundation Server communicates directly with Microsoft Project and Excel (http://techrepublic.com.com/5264-1-0.html?query=excel%20anatomy). Managed add-ins let you launch Excel or Project from Visual Studio 2005 Team Explorer and pass work item lists between them and the Team Foundation Server. This handoff occurs within the context of an open project and allows a manager to pull work item lists from the project and handle them off-line as a matter of convenience, as a spreadsheet or a project plan. (Note that in the case of Project, you need Project 2003 Pro Edition.)

5. Application designer

I've spent lots of time with BizTalk Server 2004 (http://techrepublic.com.com/5138-7343-5795137.html) and its orchestration designer, and I'm sure many have spent hours with Visio, scooting shapes around and connecting them as if doodling on a conference room whiteboard. Team System's Application Designer takes it up a notch, with the ability to integrate Windows forms apps, Web services, BizTalk orchestrations (if they're deployed as Web services), databases, ASP.NET Web services and apps, and external Web services, and generate code to implement the integration. Designs can be saved and are source-controlled.

6. Logical datacenter and data source management

The worst disasters in Web app design that we come across are usually the result of either a user-interface design that took its data source connections for granted, or vice versa. Developers are often too much about logic and wow-factor and not enough about the logistics of data access. We need to be digging deep into the network side of things if we want a clean and efficient application.

Team System's response to this problem is a Logical Datacenter Designer, which integrates clients, Web servers, SQL Servers, and any other servers into constrained, schema-driven models that permit solution architectures to truly embrace the big picture with proper attention to networking and its impact on interface with data sources. This concept is especially welcome as Web services become increasingly central to integrated application systems.

7. Software configuration management (SCM)

As projects grow more complex, the size of the disastrous pileups that result when code is poorly managed grows as well. Poor team communication makes it all the worse, and the lack of a well-constructed, high-level integration plan can lead to embarrassing compromises with requirements and user expectations, if not outright project failure. Software configuration management (SCM) is critical to project success today, and thankfully Team System includes it.

Source control is a given these days, but the extras included here are tracking of the work items and build management mentioned earlier. Work items covers tasks, bugs, requirements, risk, and the high-level scenario. These work items can be defined in your methodology (see #2) and have properties, making them rich objects for detailed project definition as you move through the development cycle. Your tracking of these items can be customized. Build management—called Team Build and based on MSBuild—gives you a build customization tool with compile, source control, unit testing, static analysis, binary routing, build reporting, and test result reporting.

8. SharePoint Services—create a team portal

More than a few IT shops are using SharePoint Services for team collaboration (http://techrepublic.com.com/5138-7343-5836611.html), for project tracking, sharing of documentation, even source control. Team System is a good fit for SharePoint. Versioning, check-in and -out, and security are built-in, and SharePoint is friendly to the other MS clients mentioned above.

9. Integrated testing

If you're going to design and implement from an architectural level, you need to be able to test from top to bottom. Unit testing we've already mentioned, but testing at the integration and system levels is usually done manually. Team System allows you to create and implement high-level tests and bug-tracking from Word templates that can be launched from Visual Studio 2005; there's still a human in the loop, but you can now give that process the continuity and depth that you have at the unit-test level. You also have a Generic Test Designer for creating tests that wrap other testing tools and record the results. You also have Web Test Recorder, which launches from Visual Studio, rus on Internet Explorer, and captures a tester's navigation when testing Web sites.

10. System Designer

Lest it seem as though the whole point of VS/TS is to immerse you in the big picture, you can take comfort in the System Designer, which breaks an integrated application down into the Smallest Deployable Unit, whatever that might be in your particular project. The idea is to keep the components of a large application system manageable—hard to do under the best of circumstances, in a multitiered system—and yet maintain project-wide continuity throughout development.

The increased granularity at the System Designer level allows you to develop and test between components forming subsystems, in the process overriding configurations and definitions at the higher project level, if need be, and then disseminating those changes at the application level. Or, if needed, you can store the overrides for later comparison and examination, until ideal deployments at the subsystem level emerge. ❖

10 things you should know about Visual Studio 2005 and the .NET Framework 2.0

By Scott Robinson

Those wacky, zany folks in Redmond send more mixed signals than anyone else in the industry, don't they? For several years, it's been unclear to what extent they would actually leverage the .NET Framework (http://techrepublic.com.com/5100-3513_11-5927257.html), and their protracted time-to-market on new versions of products makes us wonder how much indecision contaminates their development process. We're left wondering if the .NET Framework will remain an over-hyped side dish, whether Avalon will replace ASP.NET (http://techrepublic.com.com/5138-9592-5933843.html), whether any MS product will ever be more than a warmed-over version of a predecessor.

Well, they must have heard us grumbling, because the major overhaul in the Microsoft catalog announced at TechEd this summer has brought us a cornucopia of enhancements, most of them good, and many of them exactly what we asked for. One of the biggest boons is the long-awaited SQL Server 2005 (http://techrepublic.com.com/5138-9592-5823770.html). However, there are many highlights worthy of note to developers as well.

If there's one fact to keep in mind when considering the new Visual Studio 2005 (VS), it's the depth of integration between VS, the .NET Framework 2.0, and ASP.NET 2.0. The leveraging of these products into a more-or-less seamless whole is the fundamental goal of Microsoft's latest round of development. This being the case, this particular 10 things list focuses on features deriving from this integration.

1. Classes can now be passed as parameters.

Restricting array classes to types that meet an application's needs means one of two things: designing arrays that only hold types you want them to hold—cumbersome—or using generic arrays and living with the fact that they'll accept anything. The best of both worlds is to be able to use a base class array yet have a way to restrict it to types that we want. It's sort of possible to do this already, by writing wrappers for all the array class's methods, but that's a lot of blah-blah at the application logic level.

It is better to have a way of making arrays type-dynamic, so that we can tell the array that a particular object type is headed its way. You can design an array class that will accept any class desired by the client. This is done with the generic `List` class, which can accept type as a parameter, submitted by the client, and then will accept objects of that type.

2. "Generics" enables type-independent class design.

A key failing of the .NET Framework has been its lack of some analog to Java's "template" mechanism, a means of parameterizing object types and classes (C++ has a similar template feature). You now have a similar mechanism called *generics*.

Using generics, you can design a class that is type-generic, permitting you to make use of whatever type is submitted, without generating an error; you now have syntax to create a class that sees type as a parameter. Generics are language-independent, and in addition to permitting you to create your own classes, the generic mechanism is available in collection classes included with .NET Framework 2.0.

3. Deal with unmanaged garbage.

Even if all unmanaged resources are freed when they aren't needed, the fact is that garbage collection, as in real world, only happens so often. Good wrappers do nothing more than set it out on the curb to be picked up. We get into trouble with this because the collection is scheduled, rather than dynamic (at least where accumulation of unmanaged resources is concerned). Up till now, we've been able to do this manually, with the `IDisposable` interface, but now we don't have to do it ourselves.

The CLR keeps tabs on the managed heap, but the problem with unmanaged resources is that they are taken up by wrappers in the managed heap, creating a Catch-22. Wrappers begin accumulating wrapping resources that need to be made available again, without waiting for scheduled garbage collection. You can run out of space as the managed heap allots memory for the wrappers but can't provide the resources they want to wrap—and you can't wait for the next garbage collection. You need to be able to trigger the reclamation of those resources. Garbage collection has been improved by the inclusion of two new methods to deal with these problems.

`AddMemoryPressure` and `ReleaseMemoryPressure` work as follows. `AddMemoryPressure` causes garbage collection to happen more often; a managed object using a chunk of unmanaged memory will call `AddMemoryPressure`, and the collector sees the object as being of a size equally itself plus its wrapped unmanaged resources. The object then calls `ReleaseMemoryPressure` after finishing with the resources it wrapped, creating a kind of memory management equilibrium. What's particularly nice about these methods is that the methods accept a parameter allowing you to plus- or minus- the "pressure."

4. Put user authentication into apps without having to build it yourself.

Just this past week, a colleague came into my office and lamented that he would need to take a security course sometime soon because of problems he was having with a Web app. He's not alone; the biggest challenge of having to create infrastructure to manage user authentication concerns is that it is very complex, and most developers aren't trained in it (and shouldn't have to be).

It's common to respond to this problem by way of forms authentication—the application you're designing authenticates the client up-front, then cookies the client with an encrypted authentication, which it consults with each subsequent request for additional pages from the same server or group of servers. The problem was that even though you had all the tools for building such a system, you had to do exactly that—build it yourself. Now, by way of ASP.NET 2.0, we have classes provided to do most of the work.

As an extra, ASP.NET 2.0's authentication classes not only gives us built-in user account set-up and storage, password handling and look-up, but can also automatically add and retrieve user roles.

5. Manage user-based content display and user data persistence.

In addition to built-in parts for managing user roles, we are now provided with a control—`LoginView`—that allows us to set up content-by-user, displaying the pages appropriate for whoever has logged in to an app, with almost no code. In addition, we have classes giving application program access to application configuration; with this capability comes storage of user-specific data in the configuration database, so apps can easily track user data between visits to a site—again, with almost no code. This feature can even be used with anonymous users.

6. Allow user choice of application interface.

Creating Web apps and pages that give users the ability to customize is often desirable and almost invariably complex. Building infrastructure like this for individual applications is incredibly costly. The new Visual Studio suite reduces the complexity dramatically: leveraging themes for application interface (which Whidbey unfortunately demonstrated sparingly), an XML mechanism for presentation configuration is built in to the `LoginName` control. IT departments can easily put together skins that bring their Web apps into stylistic conformity with their general corporate look and feel with little mess; but the real pay-offs are simple programmatic theme application to new pages via the property `PageTheme`, and the inclusion of theme in the "personalization" database described above, enabling the inclusion of user-theme-selectability in apps with only a handful of lines of code.

7. Employ Team System.

One of the variations of the new Visual Studio .NET 2005 is Team System, a productivity suite that leverages Solutions Framework 4.0 for life-cycle development and provides efficiency tools for team activity. Built on clearly defined team member roles, it is driven by an architectural best practices paradigm, with work-item tracking, code analysis, unit testing, planned backup, UML and other features. A topic worthy of a 10 Things list in itself.

8. Gain independence from IIS, three cheers!

There are developers out there who shout at the sky, turn green, and rip their shirts over IIS. This month I watched a coworker fling dirty looks toward Washington State till nearly midnight over a permissions issue when trying to execute a Web service client that had run fine from VBScript from ASP.NET. Now we'll have a more favorable outburst over freedom from Internet Information Server.

This isn't total freedom, mind you—for final testing, we still need IIS, but we can get the bulk of our development out of the way without having to struggle with the corporate system cops over IIS installations and potential security gaps. Visual Studio 2005 can run on individual machines without IIS. We can run the apps we are working on without it, allowing most of the debug work to happen before worrying about IIS at all.

9. Utilize Web services authentication support.

Web services, like any other Web-based data transaction, usually require authentication of the users trying to access the servers upon which services reside. We usually have to address this when designing and implementing a new Web service, and it's a nuisance. Web Services Enhancements 2.0 provides classes for implementing Web service authentication support, with useful (and often business-critical) options in password-hashing, password return, and token handling, giving your VS Web services development more transport-protocol-independence than before.

10. Solve the Web services XML problem domain.

There are few more frustrating aspects to the otherwise action-packed world of IT application development today than emerging standards. XML Web Services hold incredible promise but are still very young, and common problem domain vocabulary is key. Microsoft would love to provide the standards here—they wish—but since the world isn't quite ready for that (as Passport attests), we now have the problem of selecting a standard to use when designing and implementing XML Web services.

What to do? Select a standard and code forever, turning it into an implementation? Life's too short. Until the dust settles in the critical-mass-standards for Web services showdown, we can leverage Web Services Enhancements 2.0, which lets us choose from the existing not-yet-canonized standards, downloading canned implementations, so we can get right to work with common Web services infrastructure that needs only our business logic. You can add WSE 2.0 to your Visual Studio 2005 arsenal from MSDN. ❖

10 tips for creating a successful e-commerce site

By Debra Littlejohn Shinder, MCSE, MVP

Building an e-commerce site can take your business to the next level and greatly expand your customer base, but selling successfully online requires more than just signing up with an e-commerce host and watching the money roll in. Here are some important elements of a successful e-commerce site.

1. Location, location, location

In the physical world, location refers to your city/state, the neighborhood where your business is located, the proximity of the nearest freeway, major street, or back street, etc. In the online world, location is defined by where your Web servers are: onsite at your business, with a hosting company, or with your ISP. In the case of both the physical and the online worlds, location can make all the difference, especially when it comes to the control you have over your site and its reliability. After all, a site that's down doesn't bring in any money.

2. Branding

Building a name and reputation is just as important for an online business as for a bricks-and-mortar one—maybe more so. A business name that people will retain should be coupled with a domain name that's easy to remember and come back to. Something like www.smith-cattle-herders.com is much more descriptive and memorable than www.joesmith.com (even if the latter weren't likely to be taken). Keep the domain name as short as you can while still keeping it unique and descriptive. And watch out for confusion or unintended meanings caused by combining words in a domain name. For example, John's Exchange becomes johnsexchange.com, which can also be read as "John Sex Change."

3. First impressions

The front page of your Web site is your first (and maybe last) chance to make a good first impression. An attractive site can draw in customers; a blah or unappealing site can drive them away. Logos and taglines help distinguish your site from all the others, but don't go overboard with animations and special effects. Keep it professional. Unless someone on your staff has a talent for design, it's worth the expense to pay a professional to design your site to set the stage and mood that's appropriate for your particular business and target audience. Color, fonts, graphics, and layout all determine the impression a site makes and there is no one-size-fits-all template. If the budget is tight, have the professional designer just do the front page.

4. Efficient downloading

In today's "instant gratification" society, people will click away from a site that doesn't download quickly. Make sure your Web server is on a fast connection and don't load up the graphics and other large files that take a lot of time to download. Remember that many people, especially in rural areas (who are prime candidates for buying online because they aren't near retail outlets), are still connecting via 56Kbps (or less) dialup connections.

5. Ease of use

There's nothing that will drive potential customers away faster than a site that's frustrating to navigate. If essential information is buried deep within multiple levels of a site, with no clear way to get there, you'll lose business no matter how great your product is. Navigation buttons or bars leading to most frequently needed information should be displayed on every page, and a site map, with cross-referenced links, will help site visitors find less frequently accessed information. Don't make visitors dig for crucial information. For example, include shipping charges on the pricing page; don't make customers go through the entire order process to find out what shipping will cost them. Ensure that it takes as few clicks as possible to make a purchase.

6. Information: More is better

The only thing that's more frustrating than information that's buried on an inside page is information that's missing altogether. Provide detailed specifications for each of your products. A person who's considering buying a table wants to know its size (length, width, height), whether it's made of real wood or laminate, how much assembly is required, and so forth. Anticipate common general questions and provide an FAQ to answer them. For instance, what is your return policy for defective items?

7. Easy money

Don't make it difficult for your customers to buy from you. It goes without saying that you should be set up to accept credit card payments, but don't forget about those who don't have or don't want to use credit cards, either. The more options customers have, the more likely they'll spend their money on your site instead of somewhere else. You should also have the capability to process phone or mail-in orders. Make the phone number easy to find and provide an order form that can be printed and mailed. Some folks like to do their preliminary shopping on the Web and make the final purchase in person, so if you do have physical stores, be sure you show the address(es) on your site.

8. Site security

Identity theft is a big concern, and rightly so. Customers don't want to give you sensitive information like a credit card number unless they can trust you to keep that information safe. It's not enough that you won't misuse their info; you must also show them that you won't let it fall into the hands of someone who will. Consumer trust in businesses to protect their personal info is low following numerous security breaches of large company databases. Ensure that all transactions are encrypted and use authenticated SSL digital certificates. Play up your security measures on your site.

9. Legal compliance

Check federal, state, and local laws that affect your site. Are you required to collect sales tax on the items or services you sell online? If you collect personal information, you may be required to post a privacy statement describing your policy for sharing that information.

10. A significant presence

No matter how great your site looks and how easy it is to navigate and buy, no one will spend money there unless they know you're there. Get the word out through traditional advertising, promotion, and word of mouth. Make sure the URL is featured on your business cards, letterhead, print ads, etc. Get listed in the major search engines. Exchange links with others in related businesses. Promote your site every chance you get; you never know who your next customer will be. ❖

10 useful server variables you should know for creating dynamic Web pages

By Melonfire

Every time you request a Web page, an immense amount of activity takes place behind the scenes: your request is sent to a DNS server, an IP address is found, the corresponding Web server is contacted, and the resulting data stream is decoded and rendered by your Web browser as an HTML page. In addition to the actual HTML content requested, however, the Web server also includes a number of important "server variables" in its response. These variables contain information about both the Web server environment (its name, IP address, and software) and the current script execution environment (the script name and path and the query string).

These variables are often used by clever Web developers to make their scripts more dynamic and robust. Table A outlines some of the more useful server variables that a Web server typically sends out when it responds to an HTTP request, and also explains when and how you could use each one on your Web site.

Note: Some of these variables may not be available in all Web servers.

For more information on these and other server variables, consider taking a look at the CGI 1.1 specification (http://hoohoo.ncsa.uiuc.edu/cgi/env.html).

Table A

Variable	What It Contains	What It's Useful For
HTTP_USER_AGENT	An identification string sent by the client making the request. For example: Mozilla/5.0 (Windows; U; Windows NT 5.1; en-US; rv:1.8) Gecko/20051111 Firefox/1.5.	Client detection and logging; creating code that works differently in different browsers.
HTTP_ACCEPT_ENCODING	The list of encodings the client is able to decode.	Improving transfer speeds by using GZIP encoding (for example) to compress page data.

Variable	What It Contains	What It's Useful For
REMOTE_ADDR	The IP address of the client making the request.	Obtaining the user's geographical location for targeted advertising or localized information retrieval; restricting access to specific IP addresses or groups of IP addresses.
DOCUMENT_ROOT	The server's document root directory (as defined in its configuration).	Constructing relative/absolute paths when uploading, copying, or moving files through a Web application.
SERVER_SOFTWARE	The server's signature, indicating the name and version of the server as well as any software running on it. For example: Apache/2.0.55 (Win32).	Identifying server capabilities.
QUERY_STRING	The list of variable-value pairs that follow the "?" in the requested URL.	Retrieving and parsing the variable-value pairs sent to the server via its URL.
REQUEST_METHOD	The method used to make the URL request. For example GET, POST, or PUT.	Identifying the method used to request the page, and thereby accessing the appropriate namespace for variable retrieval.
SCRIPT_NAME	The server path to the requested resource (relative to the document root).	Retrieving the name and path to the currently executing script or resource.
HTTP_ACCEPT_CHARSET	The character sets the client is able to receive.	Sending page data in a preferred character set.
REMOTE_USER	When using HTTP authentication, the username supplied for authentication.	Content personalization; credential verification.

Notes:

Printed in the United States
61198LVS00004B/157-460